Agriculture and Spirituality

AGRICULTURE AND SPIRITUALITY

Inter(agri)cultural Dialogue

Essay from the Crossroads Conference
at Wageningen Agricultural University

International Books

CIP-GEGEVENS KONINKLIJKE BIBLIOTHEEK, THE HAGUE

Agriculture

Agriculture and Spirituality : inter(agri)cultural dialogue : Essays from the Crossroads
Conference at Wageningen Agricultural University. – Utrecht : International Books
ISBN 90-6224-980-9
NUGI 615/835
Keywords: agriculture, environment, ecology, spirituality

Thanks to Niala Maharaj, Chris Rigg and Lin Pugh for correcting the English texts.

® Crossroads, 1995

Cover design: Marjo Starink, Amsterdam
Printing: Haasbeek, Alphen aan den Rijn

International Books, A. Numankade 17, 3572 KP Utrecht, the Netherlands
Tel. 31 (0)30-2731840, fax 31 (0)30-2733614

Contents

Introduction

I am honoured to introduce this booklet, which contains the three lectures from the symposium "Inter(agri)Cultural Dialogue: Agriculture and Spirituality", which was organized by Crossroads on 9 March 1994.

The theme originated at a meeting of Crossroads, an initiative of the Chaplaincy for International and Dutch students in Wageningen, the Netherlands, which began in 1991. Crossroads aims to create dialogue for students from diverse cultural religious and ideological backgrounds "to meet each other at the crossroads of our own lives and at the crossroads of world society". Wageningen is the seat of a renowned agricultural university. Crossroads tries to focus on issues of culture, religion and (world) society. So before we understood what was going on, our first Open House Meeting, on Spirituality and Agriculture, was organized. That first evening turned out to be both challenging and embarrassing. We discovered that we were not used to relating these subjects. All of us were at home in the field of religion and spirituality, while specializing in one or other area of agriculture. But linking spirituality and agriculture was strange, we realised with some discomfort; it had never been part of our main discourse. We sensed that something important was at stake and stretched our capacities to try and bridge the gap between our professional interest, agriculture, and our personal spirituality/faith.

Since then, the project, "Agriculture and Spirituality" has expanded, gained its own momentum and produced many surprises. The small conference we planned to hold in Wageningen, for instance, turned into a large symposium with 250 Dutch and international participants from all over the Netherlands. And we had to turn away many other applicants, to our regret.

This booklet is aimed, once more, to be a small step in the exploration of this field we have discovered, an attempt to help develop and restore the discourse on spirituality and agriculture. We hope that this discourse will not be confined to the realm of Western agriculture, but will open up discussion on a whole range of alliances between spirituality and agriculture in a diversity of cultural contexts. And, of course, we would like this process to renew agricultural praxis. A new link between agriculture and faith may stop the unlimited exploitation of "Mother Earth" and bring balance between agriculture and nature. We hope that agriculture and its research will not be a closed circle in itself, but will be subservient to humanity and nature/the earth. This assumes a definition of "spirituality" which refers not only to God/the Divine, but also to the struggle for human dignity, equal sharing, against exploitation of people and nature. God him/herself is fundamentally linked with the struggle for justice and wholeness. We hope for a new sense of responsibility, a new attitude of caring (caring objectivity) and a (re)new(ed) awareness that, "The earth and everything in it, the world and all who live in it, is the Lord's".

We are grateful to many people and organizations. Quite a few organizations concerned with agriculture, science and religion (churches) have been generous to this project. Without their support this symposium would have been too expensive and thus impossible. We are also indebted to the Thomas More Academy, which was excellent at developing and organizing the symposium on behalf of Crossroads. Their experience in conference organization made them indispensable.

We were very honoured to have the lecturers we did: Professor Gerrit Huizer, Dr Vandana Shiva and Dr Henk Verhoog. Their contributions make up this booklet, together with four articles closely related to its theme. As we received quite a lot of responses after the symposium, we decided to add articles by Dr Frans Verkleij, Ir Rob Witte, Wim Zweers and Dr Petran Kockelkoren. The former two are members of the Crossroads organizing committee, and Wim Zweers' article was written in response to the symposium. Only the final article was written independently of the symposium, but we chose to include it because of its links with the main contents.

We are grateful to Dr Els Postel (Interim professor Gender Studies at the Agricultural University in Wageningen) who was the chair on the day. And finally, I wish to express a word of admiration for the members of the Crossroads committee which organised the Symposium. They invested considerable energy and it was a privilege to work with them: Ruurdtje Boersma, Caspar Govaart (Thomas More Academy), Neeltje Kielen, Erna Ovaa, Frans Verkleij, Rob Witte and lastly, my colleague Marianne Schulte Kemna (Student Chaplain in Wageningen), with whom it has been a pleasure to work from the beginning.

Hinne Wagenaar, Chaplain to International Students in the Netherlands

CHAPTER 1

Indigenous Knowledge and Popular Spirituality

A Challenge to Developmentalists[1]

Gerrit Huizer

The development of modern science, reflected in Francis Bacon's idea "Knowledge is power", emerged in Europe in what turned out to be a crucial period of world history. Having shaken off Islamic influence after the fall of Granada, the Spanish had begun the extension of their power into what they thought were the Indies. While so doing, extending their worldview and decimating the local population, they brought back gold and more gold, but also a great deal of indigenous knowledge about hitherto unknown products such as potatoes, tomatoes, maize, beans and other products. Some of these are now exported from the subsidized agricultural surpluses in the West to the so-called Third World.

An important question is: Can Westerners really understand indigenous knowledge systems without adopting – or at least coming seriously to grips with – the broader (politico-religious) worldview of which these systems form an integral part? And to what extent does such adoption imply the need to transcend the paradigmatic limitations of the Western scientific worldview common since Francis Bacon? These fundamental questions cannot be definitively answered as yet, but they certainly cannot be ignored if a serious dialogue is undertaken with those who represent their form of (what *we* call) indigenous knowledge.

It has been observed by historians and anthropologists that before, as well as after, any "extension" came about, common people in all cultures had considerable experiential and empirical knowledge of their own. They developed appropriate strategies to cope more or less effectively with their natural environment for survival e.g. through agriculture and health care, based on a close participation with and dependency on natural processes, often with ritual/spiritual implications (Van den Berg 1989).

---

1 This article is an elaborated version of a paper presented at the International Workshop "Agricultural Knowledge Systems and the Role of Extension", Bad Bol/University of Hohenheim 21-24 May '91.

These survival strategies gave many large or small groups of people a certain autonomy in some parts of the world, so they have been characterized as "uncaptured peasantry" (Hyden 1980). However, in most of the world over the past centuries – since the Crusades, according to some accounts (Nederveen Pieterse 1989, Wolf 1982), but particularly since the end of the 15th century, peoples have become more interrelated through trade and conquests. West-Europeans became particularly dominant since that period, leading to what has been called the "world system" which currently prevails. The aggressive extension of this system all over the globe was facilitated by the "scientific revolution" initiated by Bacon, Descartes and Newton which gave Westerners a technological superiority in some crucial fields and also a worldview that viewed nature and people(s) as objects to be dominated and manipulated.

As Global 2000, Report to the President (of the US) (1980) indicated, 10% of the world's population in the highly developed countries (USA and W. Europe) utilizes over 60% of the world's resources, while 80% of the people (those in the so-called Third World) are left with 20% of all there is to share; a discrepancy in availability of means of 24:1 in favour of people in the Western countries (not taking into account the tremendous discrepancies in wealth and power over means of production by a small elite within the centre as well as the periphery countries). The extension of this growing disequilibrium still continues, as a result of the globalization of the world's economies and the attempted "management of interdependence" guided by World Bank and/or IMF of almost all peoples by a relatively small power elite based in the West (see Trilateral Commission 1974, Kolko 1988). This is the background of our reflections on power and knowledge.

Western Technological Dominance and People's Resistance

Vandana Shiva (1988), based on Merchant (1980) and Mies (1986) and on her activist experience in a well-known environmental protection effort, the Chipko movement in Northern India, points out that the imposition – as "development" or "modernization" – of the Western knowledge system and technology has had disastrous effects for the nature and the people there, particularly women:

"This view of science as a social and political project of modern western man is emerging from the responses of those who were defined into nature and made passive and powerless: Mother Earth, women and colonised cultures. It is from these fringes that we are beginning to discern the economic, political and cultural mechanisms that have allowed a parochial science to dominate and how mechanisms of power and violence can be eliminated for a degendered, human inclusive knowledge" (Shiva 1988: 21).

At present the Western scientific knowledge system is not only challenged by Third World and feminist authors concerned with the deteriorating relation between men (male particularly) and the natural environment, but also by new discoveries in the (natural) sciences particularly in the field of quantumphysics.

Some physicists go so far as showing a certain convergence between the most sophisticated developments in that field and certain indigenous knowledge systems and worldviews such as buddhism and taoism (Capra 1976, 1983) but these claims are not uncontested by those closely familiar with such worldviews. Goonatillake (1982: 266-273), a scientist who has himself been educated in a buddhist society, finds Capra's comparisons a bit superficial but recognizes that indeed there is considerable truth and applicability in these worldviews, too easily ignored by Western scientists the past three centuries. This recognition is confirmed in research by Le Shan (1982/1966) into the activities and attitudes of physicists, mediums and mystics. However, the challenges of physicists like Capra, Bohm and Heisenberg to the current scientific paradigms and the mechanistic (Bacon-Descartes-Newton) worldview have not yet had much influence in the social sciences, including anthropology, with the exception of the work of Gregory Bateson, as shown by Berman (1981).

Berman remarked:

"The delusion of modern thinking on alternative realities is rarely exposed. Most historical and anthropological studies of witchcraft, for example, never speculate that the massive number of witchcraft trials during the sixteenth century might have been caused by something more than mass hysteria" (1981: 94).

This "delusion" could be related to what Riesman remarks about social scientists (in his critical discussion of Carlos Castañeda's work):

"In their studies of the cultures of other people they study, they almost never think that they are learning something about the way the world really is. Rather they conceive of themselves as finding out what other people's *conceptions* of the world are" (quoted in Berman 1981, 94; emphasis in original).

Berman (1981, 94) points out that it is a mistake to treat culture and knowledge of other people – be it "premodern" thought or alchemy – merely as forms or structures that they have imposed upon a reality which Western scientists know better than they do. Berman (1981: 69-132) further shows that Bacon and particularly Newton participated actively in the tradition of alchemy and the holistic worldview (hermetism), while making the discoveries which laid the foundations of modern science, the "dis-enchantment of the world". Later Newton publicly upheld only a mechanistic wordview of a predictable and thus controllable natural environment, though he privately still endorsed the more holistic alchemists' views (Ibid., 125). During Newton's lifetime, the mechanistic worldview became strongly endorsed and enhanced by the power elites (propertied classes and the Church of England) against the "enthusiasms" (as the more holistic or animistic traditional views were called) of the many popular movements and "mystical sects" of the 1640s, which resisted the emerging dominance of the capitalist class (Berman 1981, 122 ff). The science-historian Carolyn Merchant has observed about that period:

> "The animistic concept of nature as a divine, self-active organism came to be associated with atheistical and radical libertarian ideas. Social chaos, peasant uprisings and rebellions could be fed by the assumption that individuals could understand the nature of the world for themselves and could manipulate its spirits by magic. A widespread use of popular magic to control these spirits existed at all levels of society, but particularly among the lower classes" (1980: 121).

Merchant indicates that "pantheistic" views of the sects of the 17th century were part of a radical social philosophy that promoted the establishment of an egalitarian society (Ibid., 123) but that these views were repressed, to the detriment particularly of women (see also Mies 1986). The spiritual vitality of oppressed people has manifested itself however, time and time again.

In past decades, certain emancipatory political leaders have discovered and encouraged this spiritual vitality of poor men and women to maintain faith in and struggle for a good society under adverse conditions. Working closely for years with such grassroots movements, one cannot stop oneself from becoming acquainted with and enchanted by this obvious potential (Huizer 1972, 1980). It has been documented by Lanternari (1963), Wilson (1975) and others, that Third World people's survival strategies under oppressive and "spiritless" conditions, as well as emerging liberation struggles, have been inspired or supported by spiritual survival and healing traditions based on indigenous knowledge systems, similar to those existing in 16th and 17th century Europe.

While official and institutionalized religion (Confucianism, Hinduism, Islam, Christianity) has often served to support and legitimize strongly hierarchical power relations, folk religion has often cherished what Wertheim (1974: 105-118) called "counterpoint" elements that challenge these power relations and survive for years or even centuries. When power relations finally became unbearable, these counterpoint elements have served as starting points for overthrowing or radically changing the existing order.

One of the most important revolutionary leaders of this century Mao Ze Dong (1927) discovered and consciously followed the age-old folk tradition of (mostly taoist inspired) people's rebellions in his area of origin, Hunan. He then helped the peasants' there to get better organized against overwhelming odds. In his strategic writings about organization and guerilla warfare, he used taoist and folkloric wisdom and texts as much as those of Marx and Lenin (Freiberg 1977). One of the great feats of the more than 20 years of struggle of the Chinese peasant guerilla armies was a kind of modern Exodus, the Long March in 1934-35, in which they escaped total annihilation by the overwhelmingly superior armies of Chiang Kai Shek, withdrawing through remote and inhospitable parts of China to the isolated Yenan province. Here, the numerically weakened but spiritually and morally strengthened peasant rebels could establish their base, distribute the land to the tillers and build a society based on what Edgar Snow (1968: 226) called "rural equalitarianism", which served as a base for the conquest of all of China in the late forties. As Tibor Mende (1968: 225) remarked, one of the main advantages of the Long March was:

"Like an involuntary and monumental study tour, it splendidly completed the Communists' already unrivalled knowledge of the Chinese peasant's psychology. It brought them into contact with new regions and different peoples. Disseminating their ideas among them on their way, they also learned a great deal about the problems and the attitudes of masses they were destined to govern later on. As a significant by-product of the experience, for the first time the Long March brought the Communists into direct contact with the 'national minorities' of the Southwest and of the Western regions, and rendered both sides conscious of their ideas and aims."

It is not accidental that Mao was aware that if the rebellion he guided really had to become a revolution he had to ensure the participation of women, to whom he gave great importance. In China's past women played a considerable role in rebellious or revolutionary movements. As Wolf (1969: 112) noted about the secret societies which opposed Confucianism during past centuries in China, "most of them were strongly feminist, contrary to Confucian thinking which asserted the male *yang* over the female *yin:* the secret societies tended to accord equal status to women".

These societies facilitated the entrance and orientation of the Communist Party. The Taiping Rebellion (1850-1865) had also had such feminist influences and advances in the status of women (Wolf 1969: 122-123).

As part of the revolutionary changes in China after 1949, much attention was given to the renewal of respect for Chinese indigenous knowledge and cultural values, which had been strongly dominated by Western influence since the Opium War in the first half of the 19th century. Part of this knowledge were forms of healing and medicine based on taoism, *I-Ching* and the *yin-yang* principles, such as acupuncture, moxa treatment (moxibustion), respiratory therapy and physiotherapeutic exercises *(t'ai-chi-ch'üan)* (Palos 1972: ch. 4, 5, 6 and 8). The origin of acupuncture dates back to ± 1500 B.C. and has been known about for several centuries in Western countries (e.g. through a book from 1683 by Ten Rhyne, a doctor of the Dutch East-Indies Company). Particularly during the Western-influenced Kuomintang regime, acupuncture was discredited as superstition and practically banned. Shortly after the revolution, there were about 500,000 traditionally-trained doctors in China and only 70,000 who had received any kind of scientific training. Immediately after the revolution exchange between modern and traditional medicine and careful study of the latter was encouraged. In 1955 a Traditional Chinese Medical Academy was set up in Peking. In the meantime, acupuncture is increasingly being viewed as an important addition to the regular scientific medical practices in many Western countries, where folk-healing knowledge has been branded as superstition since the witch hunts.

Ehrenreich and English (n.d.: 3) observed that also in Europe's history, folkhealers have played a highly important role "in the midst of rebellious lower class movements which have struggled to be free from the established authorities". This was noted for the medieval period as one of the reasons why millions of women were killed in the witch hunts. The lower classes in that epoch depended mainly on "witch healers" as general medical practitioners, although the Catholic Church strongly combated these empiricists, whose attitude was not "religiously passive, but actively inquiring". These women seemed to be organized to some extent, trading herbal lore and passing on experience, but were probably also connected to rebellious movements. The ruling classes and the Church launched a terror campaign against them, which was conceived mainly by the priests Krämer and Sprenger in 1487 in their book *Malleus Maleficarum* (Hammer of Witches). Ehrenreich and English (n.d.: 6) noted:

"In locale and timing the most virulent witch hunts were associated with periods of great social upheaval shaking feudalism at its roots, mass peasant uprisings and conspiracies, the beginnings of capitalism, and the rise of Protestantism. There is fragmentary evidence – which feminists ought to follow up – suggesting that in some areas witchcraft represented a female-led peasant rebellion."

Maria Mies (1986: 74-89) also shows how the emergence of early capitalism in Western Europe and of colonialism in the Third World was accompanied by ruthless oppression of women's resistance and rebellion, culminating in the witch-hunt in Europe.

It seems that in most parts of the world, class and popular resistance in the past as well as the present relied on indigenous knowledge regarding psychic and spiritual forces which were branded as occult, superstitious or even satanic by ruling ideologies (be they christian, confucian or merely capitalist). They continued, however, to appear and reappear as a "counterpoint" and part of folk-culture with a certain amount of impact until today, and are apparently being re-discovered (Huizer 1985).

In the course of many years as a development worker, I observed the confrontation between our Western knowledge system and that of indigenous peoples in the so-called non-Western world. I gradually discovered the limitations of my own Western worldview and was helped to become acquainted with dimensions of knowledge that I subsume under the rather vague and not very adequate term spirituality. This spirituality is related to the "resistance to change" that peasants', and particularly women, in non-Western societies have shown towards the Western knowledge systems that were "extended" to them by development agents, including myself for some time. Thus I found that "resistance to change" proved to be an integral part of the "indigenous knowledge system" of the peasantry in many Third World countries.

It was clear from various experiences that "indigenous knowledge systems" were different, if not contrary, to those of Western scholars considered experts in applied anthropology and development. Maslow (1966) has made a useful distinction between "experiential knowledge" and "spectator knowledge" and he stipulated the former as being a precondition for the latter. This latter is the kind of knowledge the orthodox scientist is generally looking for, neutral, quantifiable, objectified, detached and non-involved. Both kinds of knowledge complement each other, but most of present-day science has neglected the experiential knowledge which is a result of identification, of "becoming and being what is to be known, rather than remaining totally the outside spectator" (Ibid.: 50). For a real understanding, in addition to the objectivity of the spectator, a "caring objectivity" is needed, seeing the object as much as possible "in its own nature" (Ibid.: 114-118). Thus, in order to claim any measure of scientific value for my findings, I should present what Becker (1958: 659-660) called the "natural history of the conclusions", "spectator knowledge" based on "experiential knowledge", to phrase it differently.

Learning from the People's Survival Strategies

Starting in 1954, I spent most of my adult life, almost 20 years, in Third World countries, learning by trial and error about, and particularly from, people in crisis situations. During this process I gradually became acquainted with and began to share the worldview that enables men and women in such crisis situations to survive, and which, at times, inspires them to radical action. This worldview and inspiration are partly based on conscious and unconscious psychological defence mechanisms but there is often an additional dimension of "vital force" or spirituality sometimes including healing and witchcraft. It should be noted that these latter forces have not as yet been properly defined, categorised or understood by Western scientists (including myself) but is part of effective "indigenous knowledge systems".

I have tried to come to grips with such phenomena through active participation in the struggle for survival and justice of the people I got involved with as a development worker and through careful reflection upon the experiential knowledge thus acquired. This form of research can be called "research-through-action" (see Huizer 1979). In many cases, the people I worked with shared this reflexive process, making it "participatory action research" in the perspective of a "view from within and from below".

Right from the start of those twenty years of more or less intensive work with peasants, I often observed how distrustful and seemingly apathetic or fatalistic peasants were when faced with "modernizing" agents or processes, with deeply rational attitudes. (Huizer 1972: ch. 2). My first real experience with the rationality of peasant distrust occurred in 1955 when I set out to live as a voluntary community development worker in a village in El Salvador. This was after a well-intentioned and badly needed drinking water project which our agency tried to introduce failed because of the non-participation of the peasants; they did not show up to work with us. I experienced the first crisis in my developmentalist ideology. I discovered the reason for the peasants' apparent apathy only after I had actually lived in their village for some time, not really knowing what to do, but simply "hanging around" without asking too many questions (see Huizer 1965). The peasants gradually showed me how most projects, especially those where people had to "participate", to contribute with voluntary labour, usually benefited the better-off, particularly landlords, rather than themselves. So why do all the work?

After deciding for myself to relax and "wait and see", I learnt that my neighbours – though hardly any one had any formal schooling – were great and patient teachers not only in such relatively simple things as ploughing with unwilling oxen, tracing and hunting wild pigs or the use of certain herbs (which appeared to me to be just weeds). Their main lesson, not explicitly taught but implicitly communicated in our conviviality, was a shrewd analysis of the behaviour of outsiders particularly those "from above". Without ever using the term "class", they taught me, and made me feel, what "class struggle" meant to those who only have the "weapons of the weak" (Scott 1985) at their disposal. They allowed and stimulated me to share all their frequent spiritual traditional celebrations concerning life and survival, and particularly death, that appeared to help them to remain cheerful and resistant under rather desperate conditions of (mostly covert) struggle.

After I had become accepted as a neighbour and friend of the villagers, I helped organize small-scale projects with them on their own behalf, at times even confronting the local administration (within permissible limits). Thus I learnt that the villagers' distrustful view of outsiders ("those from above") were much more correct than the views of most outsiders, including myself. Peasant "apathy" and non-participation in "development"-projects initiated "from above" proved, in most cases, to be justified and based on considerable experiential knowledge of rural elite strategies. Peasants' non-participation was a rationally and consciously adopted strategy of not letting themselves be exploited more than they already were. I also learnt that under more encouraging conditions, their "apathy" could easily be transformed into enthusiastic support and considerable effort (Huizer 1972: ch. 3). Over time, I became more and more aware of the tremendous odds most peasants in Third World countries have to face due to the almost permanent crisis they are living in. I gradually came to admire their courage and endurance under such circumstances though I was also puzzled by it: how do people deal with crisis as a way of life?

There were some special experiences that struck me. While, at times, men gave up under stress and fell into the vices of alcoholism, women almost always managed to keep going. They fed and educated their children, helping each other when illness or bad luck occurred. They seemed to possess a considerable creativity in making ends meet. In spite of having to live with innumerable crises, women managed to maintain a cheerful spirit. All this is quite contrary to the way women and peasants are often pictured in the literature (see also Huizer 1986).

The men, more directly confronted with employers, authorities, landlords, merchants and others "from above", also showed, in spite of their ups and downs (like alcoholism), considerable physical and psychological endurance. On the whole, peasants took their position less for granted than outsiders (e.g. development workers like myself) thought. Those "from above" (where I also had some friends) were sufficiently aware of this potential rebelliousness to feel the need to maintain a strong military police force to keep people "in their place". Most officials carried pistols whenever they went "into the field".

During this and several other village level work experiences, I observed that there were certain people, men and women, with a special capacity to express clearly what their peers were feeling about certain crisis situations (Huizer 1972: 153-160). I learned to recognize such people as persons with *charisma*. These people radiated a "vital force", knew how to inspire others, and were respected for this. Some of them took considerable risks in serving their community. Others used their *charisma* for their own benefit.

When crisis situations became acute and confrontation with powerful people could no longer be avoided, those with *charisma* were the crucial motivators to get their peers to act against the physical and psychological power that landlords and rich farmers hold over "their" peasants. (This includes patronage as a covert form of power exercise). In this confrontation, those with established power had most of the advantages, particularly the backing of brutal force such as heavily armed policemen or private gunmen.

In trying to answer the question of what kept peasants and women going for several years I came to the conclusion that two aspects of "indigenous knowledge" were crucial:

1. A certain clarity in people's minds about those who constitute the main cause of their permanent crisis: a kind of "common enemy" or "negative reference group" (Coser 1968). This awareness is combined with a historical perspective, bridging generations, that gives them the (unspoken) conviction that, since their society had been more just and egalitarian in the past, it might or should be so in the future.

2. A permanent spiritual revitalization grounded in a (holistic) religious awareness (from both christianity and/or pre-christian indigenous religiosity) which takes for granted the continuity and one-ness of life and after-life, good and evil, natural and supernatural in a way that is difficult for Western middle-class christian-educated people like myself to understand.

These two aspects of peasants' worldview often appeared to have enough coherence to give them the strength to endure what were virtually unbearable situations to Western eyes. It sometimes prompted them to resist or rebel as happened in situations that I became intimately acquainted with in the villages where I worked in El Salvador, and later in Mexico, Northern Africa and Southern Italy. Most of the fashionable literature of anthropologists used by development workers in those years (Banfield 1958, Foster 1962, 1965; Erasmus 1961, 1968) implied that people in such environments were poor mainly because they lacked "achievement motivation" or were irrationally "fatalistic" or "apathetic". I found, through the participatory form of action research based on sharing the life of the people and discussing my findings with them, that the practical reality was the opposite of what was stated in such theories. In fact those theories confused the real issues.

Apparently the "indigenous knowledge" regarding the chances of (what outsiders called) "development" being beneficial to the peasants was different, if not the opposite of that of the knowledge of most Western experts. It took considerable time before I was sufficiently familiar with this indigenous knowledge to be able to appreciate it. The knowledge they possessed about local ways of adapting to their natural environment, e.g. coping with erosion, was solidly embedded in their knowledge of the limitations their social environment and what the "world economy" had imposed upon them e.g. in the form of coffee or sugar plantations. They were acutely aware of a contradiction between "them" (those from above) and "us". This generally means those who possess (the means of production, land) versus the dispossessed in most countries in Latin America and large parts of s.e. Asia. It means "government people", including development agents, versus "uncaptured peasants'" in many African countries.

Social Research and People's Knowledge on Power Strategies

During the early sixties the disruptive effects of "modernization" and "development" in the form of a polarization between rich and poor had become so blatantly obvious in many Third World countries that some scholars with a positivist-empirical or traditionally-religious background felt impelled to dedicate themselves to take people's knowledge, or knowing ("saber popular"), more seriously. Their efforts later became known as the "sociology of liberation" (Fals Borda 1973) and "liberation anthropology" (Frank 1969: ch. 2). Among them was the sociologist-priest Camilo Torres, who became a guerrillero after his urban people's organisation work was made impossible in the 1960's and paid for his commitment with his life. He was the precursor of what later became known as the "theology of liberation".

It was in this controversial climate that I felt encouraged to express my feelings of being offended (on behalf of the peasants) by the then fashionable theoretical concepts about peasant "subculture", for example the concepts of "amoral familism" (Banfield 1958), "image of limited good" (Foster 1965) and "encogido syndrom" (Erasmus 1968). When I re-studied the field-work of these scholars I found that they had not only misinterpreted the peasant behaviour they had "scientifically observed", but ignored factual information about latent or open peasant rebellion and political action that had taken place during their presence or shortly before their field-work in Southern Italy and Mexico (see Huizer 1970, Huizer 1972: 35-37). The ethnocentric (mis)interpretations and Western middle-class political bias in their writing were obviously contrary to people's knowledge and practice of social mobilization.

At that time, an acute crisis in social research was becoming evident through the discovery of the Camelot project in Chile, where millions of dollars (supplied by the US Defence Department) were made available to social scientists (Horowitz 1967; for a summary see Denzin 1978: 322-324). An official *Inquiry into the Ethics and Responsibilities of Social Scientists* concluded that the social scientists involved had been "extra-ordinarily naive" (Beals 1969: 6). As a result, a few anthropologists were beginning to recognize that their profession had to be "decolonialized" (Stavenhagen 1971) or "reinvented" (Hymes, 1972). Among them were anthropologists with solid experience in Latin America, like Eric Wolf (1972: 257) who denounced the "legacy of unconcern" in American anthropology and its "new vocabulary" of "imperialism", "neo-colonialism" and "internal colonialism". He observed:

"If I am correct in saying that anthropology has reached its present impasse because it has so systematically disregarded the problems of power, then we must find ways of educating ourselves in the realities of power" (1972: 261). More and more development workers, priests and social scientists were beginning to learn from the people's knowledge of power relations in a view-from-below perspective. Some of them, in the sphere of the theology of liberation, experienced this as a kind of conversion. The discovery of (or conversion to) the people's knowledge regarding their social environment, gave new vitality to grassroots development work and critical anthropology as well. Was this vitality and strength, similar to that of the peasants' survival strategy described above, related to (1) "clearness" about a "common enemy" and (2) to a holistic spiritual worldview?

As regards the "common enemy", in Hymes' (1972) pioneering anthropology reader, Eric Wolf and particularly Laura Nader argued for the need to come to grips with the question of power through what was called "studying-up" (Nader 1972): researching the power-elite strategies that to a large extent determine the life of Third World peoples. While few social scientists have pursued this issue[2], liberation theologians have (for a compilation, see Assmann 1978, Gutierrez 1979).

Development scholars, who, on the whole, have a more or less "frei-schwebende" (Mannheim) position in between social classes, have mostly looked downward, at those of socially lower status, the "underdogs", but much less or hardly at those above, the "top dogs". The circumstances of my career as a grassroots and community development worker from 1954 onward taught me to pay attention to power(holder)s in rural development, who are (often implicitly) a main focus of attention in indigenous (peasant) knowledge systems. Community development was a strategy that had become prominent in the early fifties mainly because of its impact in India, where the community development programme was initiated in 1952 with support from the Ford Foundation and the Indo-American Technical Cooperation Fund. The approach was soon adopted on a large scale and in a few years

---

2 During the 1973 Conference of the International Union of Anthropological and Ethnological Sciences at Chicago the topic was dealt with in an improvised special symposium on multinational corporations (see Idris-Soven, Idris-Soven and Vaughan 1978). It was also treated in a few contributions to the symposium on the ideology and education of anthropologists (see Huizer and Mannheim 1979 particularly the articles by June Nash, Alex Mamak and Al Gedicks).

became a nation-wide programme that was widely propagated inside and outside India (Bowles 1954: 195-214). As the US ambassador to India at that time, Chester Bowles (1954: 2), indicated:

"With China now Communist, Asia and the whole underdeveloped world would be looking to India to see if another way were possible. The Kremlin, too, would be looking to India; for long ago Lenin has said, 'The road to Paris lies through Peking and Calcutta'.

Although the Marshall Plan and related policies for European reconstruction and defence had blocked the direct path to Paris, at least for the present, even a firmly democratic Western Europe might eventually be undermined if all of Asia with its billion or more people should go the way of Communist China.

The debacle in China, which aroused such partisan argument and confusion, had virtually paralyzed American policy-making in Asia. It seemed to me that India was a place to start afresh."

Bowles was clearly in line with President Harry Truman's 1949 Inaugural Address' Point Four, the "Bold New Programme", which propagated development of what he called for the first time "underdeveloped" countries, as a "containment policy" to halt the advance of communism. This kind of US literature was widely available to development workers in the early fifties and confirmed the suspicion that I had picked up during some village-level work experiences, that development from above could be seen as a palliative to keep the peasants from achieving the changes they really wanted. It was also clear that in this context even the simplest rural development efforts as those I had been involved in were part of a global confrontation, the Cold War, Capitalism versus Communism.

During many years of work as an advisor on community organization and land reform for various UN agencies, I could observe that in many rural areas all over the Third World such (either more, or less, outspoken) contradictions and issues existed as crucial parts of the indigenous knowledge systems among the peasants concerned, men and women. In the last few years, a score of studies undertaken by the United Nations Research Institute for Social Development (UNRISD) confirm that such contradictions and awareness still prevail in many countries or have become even more acute than those prevailing in the sixties (see the summary of these UNRISD studies in Barraclough 1991).

Indigenous Knowledge and Struggle for Land

A main question related to the UN's increasing interest in structural reforms which formed part of my work in the sixties was: Why do social movements emerge in some places and become large-scale and effective and why not in others? An even more pragmatic and important question was: *how* exactly do they emerge and what can be done to stimulate or support them among supposedly "apathetic" and "ignorant" peasants.

I was to gradually learn more about the answers, not by asking these questions explicitly, but through some measure of participation and active involvement in a number of growing movements, and discussing these experiences with the people concerned and particularly activists and scholars involved in other similar movements. In addition, the growing scholarly literature in the late fifties and early sixties helped me to gain insight, analyse and systematize the concrete experiential knowledge. Generalizations about the emergence of social movements based on experiences in Latin America (Huizer 1967, 1969) were confirmed by observation and experiences with similar movements in several South-East Asian countries (for an ample discussion see Huizer 1980: 161-184). Important preconditions for social movements to emerge were in almost all instances:

1. The occurrence of a blatant and strongly felt case or situation of injustice or disadvantage (e.g. a deterioration of the actual situation or the raising of false hopes of improvement or redress).

2. The availability of able, mostly charismatic leaders who could clearly analyse the situation, voice the discontent and indicate steps for correction of grievances and inspire their peers towards action.

3. Some measure of tolerance by the state or active support from urban allies (politicians, priests, intellectuals, development workers) in coping with the effects of the state's hegemony regarding law and order.

How a movement actually emerged depended on its originally being not explicitly directed against the state but starting with demands regarding the most strongly felt concrete grievances and needs. When the elites and/or the state, instead of responding positively to the demands, tried to block the growing movement, it could well become more radical and, if violently suppressed, become revolutionary. The state loses its legitimacy by violently oppressing movements which are strongly felt to represent justified demands. Such a process of growing revolutionary struggle may take months, years or decades to come about. The struggle itself helps the peasants involved to develop from a "class-in-itself" to a "class-for-itself" and concretize or upgrade the – in many cases – traditional indigenous knowledge system regarding power-elite strategies, as happened in China in the 1930s and 1940s.

Such peasant movements were mostly forms of resistance against destruction of "life support systems" (either communal land or small farm units) to replace them by large-scale, and often ecologically and socially harmful commercial farms or plantations producing for a market. As such developments were generally supported by the state, the emerging grassroots movements against that trend often had to confront the power of the state in order to have any impact. As Barraclough (1991) and several others (Huizer 1967; Wolf 1969; Landsberger 1969) have shown, movements of peasants to defend or recover their ancestral land and livelihood have proliferated, particularly during the past century-and-a-half as a reaction to the aggressive advance of large-scale modes of production that were imposed by colonial and post-colonial economic interests, originating mainly in Western Europe and the USA. Such movements have flared up particularly since the Second World War, in some cases assuming revolutionary proportions (Wolf 1969, Huizer 1972, 1980, Barraclough 1991). This form of active participation of peasants in shaping their own fate, contributing at the same time to land reform and national development efforts, has been taken into account over the years in several UN or related publications (United Nations 1970, Barraclough 1991). But they have not been seriously considered in academic literature on rural development (Long 1977, Galjart 1982, Chambers 1983). Is this neglect because of the – to Western social scientists – controversial political nature of this form of people's participation and indigenous knowledge?

The struggle for the maintenance or recovery of a locally sustainable agriculture or forestry, against the interests of large-scale agri-business projects and enterprises, is still going on in countries like Brazil, Philippines, Colombia, India and many others, costing many lives, often ignored by the Western media (see e.g. various issues of the *Economic and Political Weekly*, published in Bombay). This has been the case particularly for a variety of "indigenous" or "aboriginal" peoples who are showing considerable endurance in the face of great odds (Peperkamp and Remie 1989). It has been documented that several official Western development agencies purposely opposed legislation or implementation of effective land reform policies (Riad El Ghonemy 1990). This, in spite of the fact that in countries with an exemplary industrial development such as Japan, Taiwan and South Korea, US policies have, in the 40s and 50s enforced or supported radical land reforms in view of popular mobilization (Huizer 1980). They thereby created a strong internal market indirectly enhancing national industrialization (Barraclough 1991).

Spirituality and Power

Of late several cases of people's mobilization under adverse conditions have drawn attention thanks to the strength of their effects. Examples are the participation of peasants in the recent liberation struggles or rural-based rebellions in countries like Zimbabwe, Nicaragua, or El Salvador. It has been documented that in these cases, spiritual/religious indigenous knowledge systems have played a more or less crucial role (see e.g. Lernoux 1982). Especially the indigenous spiritual component of the Zimbabwean liberation struggle has been amply documented (Lan 1985, Huizer 1989). Following a strategy similar to that of the peasant armies which, between 1926 and 1949, brought about the revolution in China (where many Zimbabwean freedom fighters were trained), these fighters followed the "mass-line" and let themselves be guided by indigenous spirit-mediums representing ancestral spirits cherished by the local people in the areas where the guerilla struggle was waged. This approach apparently ensured considerable effectiveness and in the Independence celebrations in 1980 the most outstanding spirit-mediums were officially honoured. As spirit-mediums have traditionally been helpful in curing illnesses and distress, solving relational problems or community conflicts and facilitating favourable environmental conditions (rain, fertility) in Zimbabwe, efforts have been proposed or implemented to study the workings of such spirit-mediums more seriously at the academic level (Chavunduka 1978, 1986). In spite of the fact that the realities concerned can hardly be understood within the paradigms of Western science, even for agricultural planning and land use, a serious consideration of these phenomena has been proposed (Hughes 1974, Schoffeleers 1978).

Traditionally, the ties between men and land in Zimbabwe, as in many other African countries, are not only material, but religious or spiritual. Land belongs to God, the ancestors and, particularly, to the founders of a lineage, clan or tribe who have been buried there. Some of the most important landmarks, certain hills, ponds, or trees, are named after ancestors whose spirits are honoured there. Every descendant is entitled to enough of this land to survive with his family. It is allotted mainly by the chief, who is the most direct

descendant of the founders of a clan and thus possesses considerable power
(Schoffeleers 1978, Introduction). Such territories of a certain tribe are guard-
ed and protected by the spirits of the ancestors who are buried there, particularly by the spirits of the oldest, founding ancestors. These are very powerful
spirits who have to guide many aspects of the daily life of the tribe in order to
keep harmony with the natural environment.

Such African indigenous knowledge also continues to play a crucial role in
modern rural development, in spite of a century or more of colonialist pene-
tration and missionary activity. Thus the Tribal Areas of Rhodesia Research
Foundation observed in a study they made in 1974 that an important factor
in traditional life in rural areas continued to be the role of the medium
("svikiro") of the "tribal spirit" ("mhondoro"). This "tribal spirit" is distinguished from the ordinary ancestor spirit ("mudzimu", pl. "vadzimu") and is
often that of the founding father of a chiefdom. Contact with these spirits is
through the medium who goes into a trance state and then speaks with the
voice of the spirit. Such "mhondoros" are particularly concerned with the
land from which their descendants derive their subsistence. As was noted by
a study on rural development projects:

> "Any planner of such a project would be wise, therefore, to acquaint him-
> self with the position with regard to these spiritual influences in the areas
> in which the project is planned to operate" (Hughes 1974: 294, see also
> Bourdillon 1982).

This study specifically recommended further investigation of the roles of
these spirit mediums in local rural development, as they could affect specific
development plans, particularly those related to land use.

It is difficult to assess to what extent there is an interaction between the
guardian spirits and the people in their territory. Schoffeleers shows how, in
various Central African societies, irregularities in the social order, such as
murder, incest, public immorality, are known to be followed by irregularities
in the ecological order, particularly droughts: management of nature depends
on the correct management and control of society. He indicates:

> "This is a profound intuition, and it is also one which is at the heart of eco-
> logical thinking in African societies. It is a concept which the industrial
> world has largely lost but which it has to restore to its rightful place if it
> desires a lasting solution to its ecological woes" (Schoffeleers 1978: 5).

Michael Gelfand (1981), who, as a medical doctor, had considerable experience in working with spirit-mediums, shows how the great majority of modern Shona people either living in urban or rural areas continue to cherish their

traditional relationships with ancestor-spirits, together with christianity. Recognition of this fact is clear from a public announcement of a body of university trained African lecturers (Sunday Mail, 19 Febr. 1978) who urged "that the university should become a centre for study, preservation, illustration and dissemination of authentic African culture and ideas" (Ibid.: 68).

Indigenous Knowledge and non-Western Cosmologies

In order to learn to appreciate the various kinds of spirit-mediumship and the role of spirits in the struggle for survival, a closer look at the cosmology of which these phenomena form part appears necessary. While, in the Western context, distinctions between the reality of science and the reality of religious practice seems to be obvious, in Africa this is much less the case (Mbiti 1970).

One of the earliest efforts to understand the cosmology and indigenous knowledge systems of Africans, particularly Bantu Africans, was the study in the mid forties by the Belgian Franciscan missionary Placide Tempels (1959), of what he called "Bantu Philosophy". During his work as a missionary, Tempels had become aware that his efforts to christianize or "civilize" the Bantus in the Congo had only a partial result and that the majority remained muntu in their heart, i.e. attached to the ancestral traditions, which were considered "childish and savage customs" by most whites. Tempels' little book, with all its paternalistic and eurocentric limitations, is now considered a kind of classic by various authors (Setiloane 1977: 62, Schoffeleers 1988: 188-190), though seriously critized by others (see below). Particularly puzzling to a missionary like Tempels (1959: 32-33) were the questions:

"How can these souls, or this force, be able, as you say, to act upon beings? How does this interaction with beings take place? How can the 'bwanga' (magical medicine, amulet, talisman) heal a man, as you say it does? How can the mfwisti, the muloji, the caster of spells, kill you, even at a distance? How can a dead man be reborn? What do you understand by this rebirth? How can the initiation ceremony turn a simple human being into a munganga, a magician healer, or, as we make him to appear later on, a master of forces? Who initiates, the man or the spirit? How does the initiate acquire 'knowledge' and 'power'? Why does a malediction have a destructive effect? How is it acquired? Why is it that our catachumens on the eve of baptism come to us and say: 'No doubt our magical cures are potent, but we wish to forswear recourse to them'?."

Tempels (1959: 330) continues, showing for his time and (missionary European) background, a rather exceptional respect for African ways:

"Such questions go beyond the usual superficial descriptions of native customs. They are not, however, fated to remain for ever unanswered. The answer to them is the one that all Bantu will make without exception. What has been called magic, animism, ancestor-worship, or dynamism – in short, all the customs of the Bantu – depend upon a single principle, knowledge of the Inmost Nature of beings, that is to say, upon their Ontological Principle. For is it not by means of this philosophical term that we must express *their knowledge of being,* of the existence of things?"

In his lifetime role of trying to change, rather than merely scientifically observe, the ways of a Bantu people, Tempels came to know the intricacies of these ways better than many anthropologists who stayed for a few years at the most, and returned to their academic chairs to elaborate their observations. As the inventor of "action research" the social psychologist Kurt Lewin once remarked: "If you want to know how things really are, just try to change them". Tempels' active involvement, combined with an exceptional open-mindedness helped somewhat to correct the – in his days – current view by Westerners that African people were "savages." He noted:

"For primitive peoples the highest wisdom consists in recognizing a unity in the order of beings in the universe from which they do not idiotically exclude a priori the spiritual world. Their whole ontology which can be systematised around the fundamental idea of 'vital force' and the associated ideas of growth, influence and vital hierarchy, reveals the world as a plurality of co-ordinated forces. This world order is the essential condition of wholeness in human beings. The Bantu add that this order comes from God and that it must be reverenced" (Ibid.: 120).

In Tempels' view, there is unity in the Bantu ontology, psychology, ethics and other aspects of what he, possibly following the Western inclination to systematize and generalize a little too much, calls Bantu philosophy as the world-view of all or most Africans. But he found the "discovery" of Bantu philosophy disconcerting (1959: 167-168). He felt impelled to question his own "civilizing" mission in Africa and discussed the concept of "civilization", benefiting from Alexis Carrel's "Man the Unknown", and pointing out:

"that our mechanical, material, industrial and – more generally – economic progress has scarcely aided the progress of humanity at all; that, on the contrary, it has contributed largely to make modern man less happy, by reason of the fact that it has misunderstood *man* and neglected him. On all sides one can hear today thoughtful people demanding that *man* should be recognized as the norm of economics and industry.

One of the best things which the Europeans have brought to Africans is their precept and example in the matter of activity. Industrialization, however, the introduction of an European economy, permanent raising of production – all that is not necessarily a measure of civilization. On the contrary, it may lead to the destruction of civilization, unless sufficient account is taken of man, of human personality" (Ibid.: 172).

Tempels' tendency to generalize (and simplify) his findings and extend them to all Bantu Africans while overlooking considerable variations has been criticized later by many (Wiredu 1984, Hountondji 1983). But his effort to start de-colonializing the Western (superiority) view of Africans as early as the forties was badly needed and appreciated by others (Irele 1983: 15-17, Idowu 1973: 101-102, Setiloane 1977:62). His critics may be right in relativizing his – in his own time provocative – ideas on African philosophy, their implicit or explicit adherence to the Western scientific views, religion or "philosophy" may in turn be relativized by the fact that the Western scientific worldview and the corresponding Bacon/Descartes/Newton inspired paradigms are now increasingly being challenged by more holistic paradigms in the physical sciences which seem to have some common ground with what Wiredu (1984) called "pre-scientific" views (see e.g. Berman 1981).

Another field where the Western post-Enlightenment science paradigm is being challenged is transpersonal psychology, particularly where it has to prove its validity in psychotherapy in transcultural situations with serious socio-economic tensions, dichotomies or culture conflict.

The South-African psychologist, Len Holdstock, has highlighted the inadequacy of Western psychology to the majority of people in South Africa, accusing it of belonging to the colonial era, with its arrogance (or ignorance?) (Holdstock 1981). He (1979) pleads for a recognition of indigenous healing and its implicit holistic approach, as a great potential. Some studies have indicated that the therapeutic efficacy of indigenous healers was often superior to that of psychiatrists, psychotherapists, or medical doctors in the treatment of certain conditions (Ibid.: 120). He also observed (Ibid.: 119):

"It is safe to assume that spiritual values and belief systems will play an ever-increasing role in the lives of that segment of the black population most adversely affected emotionally by the political superstructure. Support for this assumption derives from the ever increasing number of indigenous healers in townships like Soweto. They regard the growing incidence of indigenous healing as a manifestation of the lack of official recognition of the spiritual dimension in their lives. It is the way in which the ancestral spirits call attention to an unrecognized dimension in the lives of their 'children'."

In a recent book on education in South Africa, Holdstock (1987: 226-228) clearly recognizes that Africans can teach Westerners a great deal about the "oneness with all things". The holistic worldview, prevalent among Africans, may have provided inspiration years ago for scholars like Jan Smuts, *Holism and Evolution* (1927). Holdstock (Ibid.: 46 ff.) also shows that such holism is part of new developments in the sciences (quantum physics, relativity theory and holography) which transcend the mechanistic Newtonian worldview that has dominated Western sciences up to recently (see also above and Berman 1981).

In this context, however, it should not be forgotten that taking African indigenous knowledge systems seriously implies more than just adhering to holism as a philosophy. It needs to be explicitly related to the context of power contradictions of which it – implicitly – forms part. Also in this realm there are considerable and painful paradoxes, as pointed out by Frantz Fanon since 1952. Commenting on Tempels' book (and the preface to it by Alioune Diop), Fanon (1967/1952: 184) remarked:

"When there is no longer a 'human minimum', there is no culture. It matters very little to me to know that 'Muntu means Power' among the Bantu – or at least it might have interested me if certain details had not held me back. What use are reflections on Bantu ontology when one reads elsewhere:

'When 75,000 black miners went on strike in 1946, the state police forced them back to work by firing on them with rifles and charging with fixed bayonets. Twenty-five were killed and thousands were wounded.

At that time Smuts was the head of the government and a delegate to the Peace Conference. On farms owned by white men, the black labourers live almost like serfs'."

Struggle for a whole human life for all oppressed human beings was the main theme of Fanon's later book *"The Wretched of the Earth"*. Himself a psychiatrist and participant in the liberation struggle in Algeria, a "peasant war" (Wolf 1969) that cost about 1 million lives, Fanon knew from experience the power of knowledge and (French) technological superiority, but also the "unusual potentiality" of peasants and women to rebel, to liberate themselves after long decades of suffering oppression.

Combinations of recovering indigenous cosmology and utilizing these to guide and enhance the "empowerment" of peasant men and women are being tried out in various parts of Africa, as can be seen from the Zimbabwe experience described above and alternative people's development projects in Kenya (see e.g. Kronenburg 1988). Also in other continents indigenous knowledge and empowerment strategies are combined in participatory projects (Gianotten and De Wit 1985, Risseeuw 1989).

Concluding Remarks

Non-Western indigenous knowledge systems are, in the main, not pure, traditional ways of doing things in the days before Westerners came around, but rather part of survival and resistance strategies to avoid or to cope with the Western ways that were often aggressively imposed. Taussig (1980, 1987), Silverblatt (1987) and Farriss (1984) demonstrate this in considerable detail. Knowledge-systems cannot be seen out of the context of the mode of production (or exploitation) in which they function. Particularly Farriss (1984: 7-9) shows that the Maya knowledge systems survived in part thanks to "creative adaptation" to colonial rule:

"The Maya conceived of survival as a collective enterprise in which man, nature and the gods are all linked through mutually sustaining bonds of reciprocity, ritually forged through sacrifice and communion."

It is probably not accidental that the areas concerned in South- and Central America have been centres of endemic peasant rebellion until today.

Various authors, mostly feminists, have pointed out that there is a correlation between passive or active (political) resistance against Western-style development and the conservation and revival of authentic and sustainable (self)-development strategies and knowledge systems that take into account a less manipulative and more "participatory" approach to nature (Colgrave 1977, Mies 1986, Von Werlhof 1985, Shiva 1988).

China is a country where this strategy has been successful on a large scale, and it involves about 20% of mankind, which means twice as many people as the Western countries together. The most important aspects of the success of China's socialist economic development, as depicted by the World Bank (1983), are the redistribution of the relatively scarce agricultural land to the tillers. Later, they were brought together into cooperatives, collectives and communes to ensure an optimal and particularly sustainable agriculture in a country with about the lowest hectarage of agricultural land available per capita. Soil conservation, reafforestation and water-management could be undertaken by collective effort. Indigenous knowledge regarding local surroundings was merged with useful elements of modern Western technology ("walking on two legs") in agriculture as well as environmental and health care. The barefoot-doctor system has even been taken over by the WHO as "primary health care", to be spread all over the world. Recently the Australian environmentalist Bill Mollison commented at Wageningen Agricultural University that the Chinese are the only people who succeeded in avoiding the dead end road of Western agribusiness by using renewable resources, regional self-sufficiency and involving people and their knowledge (Wagenings Universiteitsblad 26.10.89).

This strategy of redistribution and care of essential natural assets and people laid the foundation for an average industrial growth of 10% per year between 1952-1979, in spite of the disastrous effects of the ill-fated Great Leap Forward and Cultural Revolution (World Bank 1983, I: 117). It also resulted in relatively high life expectancy in China, 10-15 years higher than that of large Asian countries with a similar per capita GNP in that period, such as India and Indonesia (World Bank 1983, III: 26 for comparative statistics). The Chinese experience appears to confirm the effectiveness of using indigenous knowledge systems regarding local power relations, as well as those regarding the natural environment, and probably deserves more serious Western consideration by developmentalists as an alternative to the hitherto-practised, rather unsuccessful (one or two "lost decades") Western strategies in other parts of the Third World.

In view of the ecological disasters that Western "development" has brought about in many Third World countries through deforestation and introduction of monocultures for the world market (Redclift 1984) now – after all – increasing attention is being given to the ecological wisdom and indigenous science still available among exploited peoples. More holistic ways than the purely objectifying and rather mechanistic approaches that have predominated in past decades are now considered seriously by Western scientists, though only rarely in a participatory manner (Shiva 1988, Esteva 1987).

A question that should be raised is to what extent Western development agencies, such as the World Bank, can utilize such alternative approaches to merely soften the worst effects of their structural adjustment policies without significantly modifying their rather destructive overall trend towards integration of every corner of the world into the global "free" market. Or is there perhaps a new openness, a Western perestroika towards a truly effective alternative? It is interesting to note that the great advocates of adjustment to the global market economy, Robert McNamara (formerly World Bank, later Royal Dutch Shell) and Johannes Witteveen (formerly IMF, currently also Royal Dutch Shell) are actively and publicly involved in currents or institutions of the so-called New Age movement that promote challenges to prevailing Western science paradigms in different fields. Is this a hopeful or an ominous sign?

It may be recommendable for Western scientists, in addition to searching for new knowledge from indigenous peoples, to carefully study their own place in the overall context of Western "development" interests in order to ensure that they really serve the interests of those from whom they are gaining new insights and inspiration.

References

Assmann, Hugo (ed.) 1978 Carter y la Logica del Imperialismo, Tomo I y II, San José, Costa Rica: Editorial Universitaria Centroamericana (EDUCA).

Banfield, Edward 1958 The Moral Basis of Backward Society, Glencoe: The Free Press.

Barraclough, Solon 1989 Social Origins of Food Policy and Hunger. Geneva: UNRISD/London: Zed Press, mimeogr. report.

Barraclough, Solon 1991 An End To Hunger? The Social Origins of Food Strategies. London: Zed Books.

Beals, Ralph 1968 Politics of Research: an Inquiry into the Ethics and Responsabilities of Social Scientists. Chicago: Aldine.

Berg, Hans v. d. 1989 La Tierra no Da Asi no Mas: Los Ritos Agricolas en la Religion de los AymaraCristianos. Amsterdam: CELDA Latin America Studies no 51.

Berman, Morris 1981 The Reenchantment of the World. Ithaca: Cornell University Press.

Bourdillon, Michael 1982 The Shona Peoples. Gweru: Mambo Press, (rev. edition).

Bowles, Chester 1954 Ambassador's Report. New York: Harper & Brothers.

Capra, Fritjof 1976 The Tao of Physics. Berkeley: Shambhala.

Capra, Fritjof 1983 The Turning Point: Science, Society and the Rising Culture. New York: Bantam.

Chambers, Robert 1983 Rural Development. Putting the last First. London: Longman.

Chavunduka, Gordon 1978 Traditional Healers and the Shona Patient, Gwelo: Mambo Press.

Chavunduka, Gordon 1986 "The organization of traditional medicine in Zimbabwe", in Last and Chavunduka, ed.(1986).

Colgrave, Sukie 1979 The Spirit of the Valley: Androgyny and Chinese Thought. London: Virago.

Coser, Lewis A. 1968 The Functions of Social Conflict. Glencoe: Free Press.

Denzin, Norman K. 1978 The Research Act. A theoretical Introduction to Sociological Methods (2nd ed.). New York: Mc Graw Hill.

Ehrenreich, Barbara and Deirdre English (z.j.) Witches, Midwives and Nurses. A
    History of Women Healers. Oyster Bay, New York: Glass Mountain Press.
Erasmus, Charles J. 1961 Man Takes Control, Cultural Development and American Aid,
    Minneapolis: University of Minnesota Press.
Erasmus, Charles J. 1968 "Community Development and the encogido syndrome",
    Human Organization, 27, 1.
Esteva, Gustavo 1987 "Regenerating people's space". In: S.N. Mendlowitz and R.B.J.
    Walker, Towards a Just World Peace: Perspectives from Social Movements. London:
    Butterworth.
Fals Borda, Orlando 1973 Ciencia Propia y Colonialismo Intelectual, (3a edicion).
    Mexico: Ed. Nuestro Tiempo.
Fanon, Frantz 1967 The Wretched of the Earth. Harmondsworth: Penguin Books (or. in
    French 1961).
Farriss, Nancy M. 1984 Maya Society under Colonial Rule. The Collective Enterprise of
    Survival. Princeton: Princeton University Press.
Foster, George M. 1962 Traditional Cultures and the Impact of Technological Change,
    New York: Harper & Brothers.
Foster, George M. 1965 "Peasant Society and the Image of limited Good", American
    Anthropologist, 67, 2.
Frank, André Gunder 1969 Latin America: Underdevelopment or Revolution. New
    York: Monthly Review Press.
Freiberg, J.W. 1977 "The dialectics in China: Maoist and Daoist". In: Bulletin of
    Concerned Asian Scholars, IX, Jan.-March, 1.
Galjart, Benno c.s. 1982 Participatie, toegang tot ontwikkeling. Leiden: Rijksuniversiteit.
Gelfand, Michael 1981 Ukama, Reflections on Shona and Western Cultures in
    Zimbabwe. Gwelo: Mambo Press.
Goonatillake, Susantha 1982 Crippled Minds. An Exploration into Colonial Culture.
    New Dehli: Vikas.
Gutierrez, Gustavo 1979 La Fuerza Historica de los Pobres. Lima: CEP.
Holdstock, T.L. 1979 "Indigenous Healing in South Africa: A neglected potential". In:
    South-African Journal of Psychology, 9, (118-124).
Holdstock, T.L. 1981 "Psychology in South-Africa belongs to the colonial era. Arrogance
    or innorance?". In: South African Journal of Psychology, 11, 4, p. 123-129.
Holdstock, T.L. 1987 Education for a New Nation. Sandton (South Africa), Media
    House Publ./Africa Transpersonal Association.
Horowitz, Irving-Louis, editor 1967 The Rise and Fall of project Camelot, Cambridge,
    Mass.: Massachusetts Institute of Technology Press.
Hountondji, Paulin J. 1983 African Philosophy: Myth and Reality. London: Hutchinson.
Hughes, A.J.B. 1974 Development in Rhodesian Tribal Areas. Salisbury: Tribal Areas of
    Rhodesian Foundation.
Huizer, G. and B. Mannheim, editors 1979 The Politics of Anthropology: From
    Colonialism and Sexism towards a View from Below. The Hague-Paris: Mouton.
Huizer, Gerrit 1965 "Evaluating community development at the grassroots: observations
    on methodology". In: America Indigena, XXV, 1965, 3.

Huizer, Gerrit 1967 On Peasant Unrest in Latin America. Washington D.C. ILO-Comite Interamericano de Desarrollo Agricola.

Huizer, Gerrit 1969 "Community Development, Land Reform and Political Participation". In: The American Journal of Economics and Sociology, 28, April, 2, p. 159-178.

Huizer, Gerrit 1970 'Resistance to change' and radical peasant mobilization: Foster and Erasmus reconsidered", Human Organization 79, 4, 1970.

Huizer, Gerrit 1972 The Revolutionary Potential of Peasants in Latin America. Lexington, Mass. Heath-Lexington Books.

Huizer, Gerrit 1973 Peasant Rebellion in Latin America. Harmondsworth: Penguin Books; republished in India, New Delhi: Marwah Publ., 1978.

Huizer, Gerrit 1979 "Research-through-action: Experiences with peasant organizations". In: Huizer and Mannheim, eds.

Huizer, Gerrit 1980 Peasant Movements and their Counterforces in South-East Asia. New Delhi: Marwah Publ.

Huizer, Gerrit 1985 "Spirituality against Oppression: Strength or Weakness of the Poor?". In: Third World Book Review, 1, 4-5.

Huizer, Gerrit 1985 "La Religion como fuente de resistencia entre los pueblos nativos de Norte-America: una vision general". In: America Indigena, XLV, Oct.-Dic. 4, 1985a.

Huizer, Gerrit 1986 "Women in resistance and research: potential against power", In: Leela Dube, Eleanor Leacock and Shirley Ardener, editors. Visibility and Power. Essays on Women in Society and Development, Delhi: Oxford University Press.

Huizer, Gerrit 1989 "Religion and the Struggle for land in Zimbabwe". In: Peperkamp and C. Remie (eds), The Struggle for Land World-wide. Saarbrücken-Fort Lauderdale: Breitenbach.

Hyden, Goran 1980 Beyond Ujamaa in Tanzania. Underdevelopment and an Uncaptured Peasantry. London: Heinemann.

Hymes, Dell, ed. 1972 Reinventing Anthropology, New York: Vintage Books.

Idowu, E.B. 1973 African Traditional Religion. New York: Orbis Books.

Irele, Abiola 1983 "Introduction". In: P. Hountondji (1983).

Kessel, Joop van 1990 "Herwaarderen om te herleven: produktieritueel en technologisch betoog bij de Andes volken". In: Derde Wereld, 9, 1/2.

Kolko, Gabriel 1988 Confronting the Third World. United States Foreign Policy 1945-1980. New York: Pantheon/Quezon City: Karrel.

Kronenburg, Jos 1988 Empowerment of the Poor. A Comparative Analysis of two Development Endeavours in Kenya. Amsterdam/Nijmegen: KIT/DWC.

Lan, David 1985 Guns and Rain. Guerrillas and Spirit Mediums in Zimbabwe. London: James Currey: Berkeley: University of California Press.

Landsberger, Henry A., ed. 1969 Latin American Peasant Movements. Ithaca: Cornell University Press.

Lanternari, Vittorio 1963 The Religions of the Oppressed. A Study of Modern Messianic Cults, London: Mc Gibbon Kee.

Last, Murray and G.L. Chavunduka, editors 1986 The Professionalization of African Medicine, Manchester: Manchester University Press (International African Institute).

Lernoux, Penny 1982 Cry of the People. The Struggle for Human Rights in Latin America – The Catholic Church in Conflict with US Policy. Harmondsworth: Penguin Books, 1980/82.

LeShan, Lawrence 1982 The Medium, the Mystic and the Physicist. Towards a General Theory of the ParaBroodtekst, (Third Printing; or.: 1966). New York: Ballantine Books.

Long, Norman 1977 An Introduction to the Sociology of Rural Development. London: Tavistock Publ.

Mao Ze Dong 1971 "Report on an Investigation of the Peasant Movements in Hunan". In: Selected Readings from the works of Mao Ze Dong. Peking: Foreign Language Press.

Maslow, Abraham H. 1966 The Psychology of Science, New York: Harper and Row.

Mbiti, John S. 1970 African Religions and Philosophy. New York: Doubleday/Anchor Books.

Mende, Tibor 1968 "The long march to Yenan". In: Schurmann and Schell, editors.

Merchant, Carolyn 1980 The Death of Nature. Women, Ecology and the Scientific Revolution. San Francisco: Harper and Row.

Mies, Maria 1986 Patriarchy and Accumulation of Capital on a World Scale. Women in the International Division of Labour. London: Zed Books.

Nader, Laora 1972 "Up the anthropologist – perspectives gained from studing up", in: Hymes, ed., 1972.

Nederveen Pieterse, Jan 1989 Empire and Emancipation. Studies in Power and Liberation on a World Scale. New York: Praeger.

Palos, Stephan 1972 The Chinese Art of Healing. New York: Bantam Books, (or. Hungarian ed. 1963).

Peperkamp, G. and C. Remi, editors 1989 The Struggle for Land World-wide. Saarbrücken – Fort Lauderdale: Breitenbach.

Ranger, T.O. 1967 Revolt in Southern Rhodesia 1896-7; A Study in African Resistance. London: Heinemann.

Redclift, Michael 1984 Development and the Environmental Crisis. Red or Green Alternatives? London/New York: Methuen.

Riad El Ghonemy, M. 1990 The Political Economy of Rural Poverty. The Case for Land Reform. London: Routlegde.

Risseeuw, Carla 1988 The Fish Don't Talk About The Water: Gender Transformation, Power and Resistance among Women in Sri Lanka. Leiden: Brill.

Schoffeleers, J.M., ed. 1978 Guardians of the Land. Essays on Central African Territorial Cults. Gwelo: Mambo Press.

Schoffeleers, Matthew 1988 "Theological styles and revolutionary elan: an African discussion". in: Philip Quarles van Ufford and Mathew Schoffeleers, eds., Religion and Development. Towards an Integrated Approach, Amsterdam: Free University Press.

Scott, James C. 1985 Weapons of the Weak. Everyday Forms of Peasant Resistance. New Haven/London: Yale University Press.

Setiloane, Gabriel M. 1976 The Image of God among the Sotho-Tswana. Rotterdam: Balkema.

Setiloane, Gabriel M. 1978 "How the traditional world-view persists in the Christianity of the Sotho-Iswana". In: E. Fasholé-Luke c.s., eds., Christianity in Independent Africa. London: Rex Collings.

Shiva, Vandana 1988 Staying Alive: Women, Ecology and Survival in India. New Delhi: Kali for Women/London: Zed Press.

Silverblatt, Irene 1987 Moon, Sun and Witches. Gender Ideologies and Class in Inca and Colonial Peru. Princeton: Princeton University Press.

Snow, Edgar 1968 "Soviet Society". In: Schurmann and Schell, editors.

Stavenhagen, Rodolfo 1971 "Decolonializing Applied Social Sciences", Human Organization, 30, 4.

Taussig, Michael 1980 The Devil and Commodity Fetishism in South America. Chapel Hill: University of North Carolina Press.

Taussig, Michael 1987 Shamanism, Colonialism and the Wild Man. A Study in Terror and Healing. Chicago/London: University of Chicago Press.

Tempels, Placide 1959 Bantu Philosophy. Paris: Presence Africaine, (Or.in Dutch, 1946).

Trilateral Commission 1974 A Turning Point in North-South Relations (prepared by Richard N. Gardner, Saburo Okita and B.J. Udink). In: Triangle Papers. New York: New York University Press, 1973/77.

United Nations 1970 Progess in Land Reform, Fifth Report. New York: United Nations.

Von Werlhof, Claudia 1985 Wenn die Bauern wiederkommen. Frauen, Arbeit und Agrobusiness in Venezuela. Bremen: Edition CON.

Wertheim, W.F. 1974 Evolution and Revolution. The Rising Waves of Emancipation. Harmondsworth: Penguin Books.

Wilson, Bryan 1975 Magic and the Millenium: Religious Movements of Protest among Tribal and Third World Peoples, Frogmore, Paladin.

Wiredu, K. (J.E.) 1984 "How not to compare African Thought with western Thought". In: Richard Wright, ed., African Philosophy. An Introduction. Third Edition. Lanham/New York/London: University Press of America.

Wolf, Eric 1969 Peasant Wars of the Twentieth Century. New York: Harper and Row.

Wolf, Eric 1972 "American anthropologists and American Society", in Hymes, ed., 1972.

Wolf, Eric 1982 Europe and the Peoples Without History, Berkeley/Los Angeles/London: University of California Press.

World Bank 1983 China. Socialist Economic Development, 3 vol. Washington, D.C. World Bank.

World Commission on Environment and Development (WCED) 1987 Our Common Future. Oxford/New York: Oxford University Press, (Brundtland Report).

CHAPTER 2

Nature, Creativity and the Arrogance of Patenting Life-forms

Vandana Shiva

This presentation began with the showing of the video, "Staying Alive", which focused on indigenous agricultural knowledge of women-farmers in India. The video shows how they select seeds for planting based on generations of effort and knowledge which is connected to their communities" worldview, spirituality, rituals and practices. By contrast, international agro-business companies try to monopolize seed, propagation material and local technologies, in order to obtain patents and sell the work of many generations for their own profit.

When the filmmaker Mira Diman came to me, saying, "I want to make a film about your book, 'Staying Alive'", I said, "No, you don't make a film on Staying Alive, you make a film on the women who have inspired Staying Alive".

She asked, "Where will I find them?"

I said, "Any village of the country".

I was requested to reflect on agriculture and spirituality, and the relationship between nature and the divine. One thing that came through very clearly for me, the more I interacted with the diverse communities in India, is that there is no way that you can say: "This is India". You will always find a part of India that is not that way. So you can never make grand theories about complex cultures. But the one thing that has come through to me again and again in the diversity of Indian cosmologies is that "the divine is nature". The divine does not make nature. And this is the reason why you will find the neem tree as a goddess itself, the soil and the earth as the goddess, and a goddess of wealth. We actually have festivals, particular festivals around November, where we have a whole day just to celebrate cow dung, as a source of wealth, as it links in with the cycle of renewability. I do not know how many festivals we have for the cow itself, to worship the cow.

If you go one step deeper, that is what "precriti" means, nature, the word for nature in most languages in India, derived from Sanskrit, which means the original activating force. It is also the word for nature, the word for creativity. Creativity and creation is not seen as something constructed as a machine by an outside maker. It is the inner drive, the inward growth of every aspect of life, in all its diversity. The fertility of the soil, the reproductive capacity of biological organisms, the renewability of water, anything that lives.

And soil, water and mountains also live. Our most important temples are temples at the sources of rivers. Even small streams always have a shrine. The four pilgrim places that, as a good Hindu, you should visit are the four tributaries of the Ganges, called the "khardahams".

This is a different view from Western cosmology, in which God the maker stands outside and gives rise to creation. I do not know enough about the religious aspects of that cosmology. I know a lot about science as a religion, developing that cosmology.

In Western cosmology, the really big break has been a shift from "God the maker, creating the world", with bits and pieces, where the bits and pieces have no intrinsic life or movement of their own, into "man the maker". And so, during the scientific revolution, we see the language of God as the "watchmaker, fixing the world like a machine". Just take a book on genetic engineering off the shelf and you will read of "the blind watchmaker", whom we no longer need.

As religion representing an ordering of the world with God as the creator gives way to science as a religion, we also see a shift from God to scientific and technocratic men as creators. The conflict clearly expressed in the film is between Indian culture and Western scientific culture. The latter assumes that the world is like a Lego set to be put together in bits and pieces, the more ostentatious you are in putting it together, the better a creator you are. It is like the kid who made the biggest truck with the Lego set.

The Indian view sees self-organization as built into life itself; it is the very definition of life. And the respect for that self-organization is what divinity is about. It is about having reverence for all life, recognizing that life is not made. It evolves, it grows, even in dying it is giving birth anew, as the seed does.

The intrinsic inner drive is also closely related to the notion of intrinsic worth. If the tree has intrinsic worth, you have reverence for it, and it is easy for you to respect the inner capacity of diverse species. Every act of human beings is tempered by that awareness of inner organization, the self-organization of diversity, and the intrinsic worth that such self-organizing capacity gives rise to. If the world is a Lego set, just fixed together, like bits of a machine, or bits of a watch, there are really no limits. There is no difference in terms of actions you take with respect to these pieces and parts of the machine, that have no dynamism, movement, meaning or worth in themselves.

Confrontation of World Views

The first round of this technocratic view of a mechanical world entered our agriculture with the green revolution. It entered the West in between the two World Wars. In my view, one of the best writings about the shift from an organic view of the world to a mechanistic view of the world as a basis for agriculture is Sir Alfred Howard's "The agricultural testament". Howard was the British Imperial agriculturalist who had been sent to India to improve Indian agriculture. He came with spray-guns, pesticides and chemicals. But when he looked around, he realized that peasant farmers had no pests. Unlike other scientists who go there and spray anyway and so create pests, he stopped and wondered why. And he found out that the type of agriculture ensures that pests do not increase beyond certain thresholds. He actually started to shift his direction, as he says in his book, "I started to treat the peasants and the pests as my teachers". Peasants and pests are not the enemies to be annihilated, but the spraygun.

As you all know, coming from agricultural systems yourselves, the green revolution shifted the view of a plant as having its own self-organization, with very intimate relationships with other aspects of the ecosystem. The plant, as any textbook on plant breeding will show you, is just a machine, and you as a breeder just have to improve that machine. From the outside, you can only improve a machine according to how you want to use it. It is necessarily linked to instrumentality. So, the plants were made short, dwarf varieties, so that they could take up more chemicals, because the idea was to sell more chemicals. The dwarf varieties were then called miracle varieties, and scientists were sent out into the world to propagate these miracle varieties. In India they were nicknamed weed-fighters.

In this language, you can see that God is disappearing, and man taking over. However religion has not disappeared. It has merely moved into science. Science itself becomes the new religion, not to be evaluated, not to be assessed, just to be believed. Scientists become priests at the altar, with no questions asked. This image is the opposite of our popular view of sciences, as an open mind, as a questioning spirit, as change, as falsification and verification. None of that has really worked. We are now going the next step, into the mechanical universe, a mechanical universe that we are putting together. God as a watchmaker who went blind, who put the world together imperfectly, and we will put it right.

The debates that are being addressed by peasants everywhere in the world, are debates that ensue from two so-called "breakthroughs", though they are essentially building on the old cosmology. Technologically, earlier in the green revolution, all you did was cross-breeding. You still allowed evolution to decide which crop could be crossed with what, and you could not cross between species" barriers. Plants had to be close relatives, varieties had to be closely related.

Now, the new tools of genetic engineering allow evolutionary barriers to be crossed, so that chickens can be crossed with potatoes, and fire-flies with tobacco-plants, so that the agro-businessman can watch his tobacco-plants glow at night. Sheep, pigs and cows can be changed and intermixed, no longer just sheep, pigs and cows, but manipulated into many things.

Why is it that the cow is seen as holy in India? The cow renews fertility, the cow gives us food, so we prefer dairy production rather than meat. Over centuries, an ecological balance has been reached. At the end of its days the cow gives us hide to make shoes and slippers. Every bit of the cow is useful. It also gives us animal traction as well as permanent fuel, it is then a renewable energy without any danger of climate change. I do not believe in the least in the problem of cows and methane. If they are offered the wrong food, they may produce enormous amounts of methane that does imbalance the ecosystem. The cows that give rise to all of this are threatened, since cows are no longer even dairy cows. Herman, the genetically-manipulated bull, is meant to be the father of 50,000 cows a year, so that those 50,000 cows can produce human protein, instead of bovine protein. Then mothers' milk will come from the cow. This, then, is supposed to be natural. For us in India this is a beautiful campaign issue. You may remember this big campaign against baby-food we had, and against the hazards of baby-food. So the food industry now answers with mothers' milk, from Herman and his 50,000 offspring. Nobody mentions the danger of genetic uniformity, toxins or hormones. Likewise poor Tracey, the sheep, is only producing proteins for the pharmaceutical industry. The language for organisms that should have intrinsic worth, is being reduced to "bio-reactors". Organisms are merely bio-reactors, to produce what we want.

Patenting Life-forms

This is closely linked to another arrogance that is being expressed in the legal field, where ideas of ownership and creation are being defined anew. If you are the creator, you can own. And when Tracey's genetic structure has been altered slightly to increase production of those proteins interesting for the pharmaceutical industry, it is then assumed that all of Tracey is created by the scientists. They have the right to go to the patent office and say "I made this".

You only get a patent for what you make. So if you get a patent for Tracey, you have the arrogance to believe that not only did you take with sophisticated instruments a gene from here and put it there, but you then have created the complex organism, into which you have fitted it. By moving a part, the entire organic whole becomes property, not just Tracey, but her offspring for 20 generations, because that is the term of the patent. One act of powerful instrumentality is leading to a world-view that assumes that protein synthesis and Tracey's capacity to produce future generations is the creation of the individual who had the capital to buy that sophisticated instrument, to go to the patent office and acquire the patent.

Patents on life are statements of man as creator. They give us an amazing opportunity for a fruitful and creative cross-cultural dialogue, an opportunity to remember where creativity belongs. What is intrinsic worth? What is the integrity of species? Basic questions that are related, not just to the freedom of diverse species, but to the very freedom and survival of the kind of people you saw in the video.

We had to spend a lot of time to define anew what it is that we are struggling for. In meetings with peasants we worked out the seed movement and the seed-campaign. In Ghandi's language, we said "It is not our right to own seed we are fighting for". Seed cannot be owned; seed is made by itself. We work with it to change its characteristics to suit us. The language of the struggle is "seed freedom", which is a combination of the freedom of the seed and the freedom of those who depend on the seed, very different from the kind of freedom that is being articulated in patents, rights to intellectual property, the double-speak of free-trade, and all the forms of manipulative power and monopolizing power that I have mentioned.

CHAPTER 3

The Oppressed Tradition of Caring Objectivity in Western Culture

Henk Verhoog

It is always difficult to speak after a speaker like Vandana Shiva. It is a great honour that I may speak here alongside such eminent speakers, whom I did not know before I was invited to talk at this symposium. Both Vandana Shiva and Gerrit Huizer described the spread of the dominant Western world view, which sees nature and sometimes people as objects to be controlled and manipulated. This attitude has often led to destructive ecological, cultural and social effects. Both Vandana Shiva and Gerrit Huizer challenge the dualistic way of thinking underlying this world view. In his paper, Gerrit Huizer speaks about Maslow's distinction between spectator knowledge of Western science against experiential knowledge of indigenous knowledge systems. The former excludes spirituality; the latter includes it in nature. Huizer describes experiential knowledge as the result of a process of identification: becoming and being what is known, a form of caring objectivity, taking care.

What I intend to show is that there is a tradition of caring objectivity in Western culture, which has been suppressed by modern experimental natural science. This tradition may be called the phenomenological way of reading the book of nature. This tradition can be recognized to some extent in what is now called organic or ecological farming, in the deep-ecology movement and in eco-theology, three developments in our culture which could have a much greater impact if they joined hands. Finally I want to point out that revitalization of the tradition of caring objectivity is a main issue for an inter-agri-cultural dialogue about agriculture and spirituality. Modern science has gained the status of a materialistic world view, or even a religion, to quote Vandana Shiva. It is often forgotten that the experimental method of modern natural science can neither deny nor confirm the existence of a spiritual world. It deliberately limits itself to what can be tested with experimental methods and so every successful experiment confirms the materialistic assumptions of natural science. Thus believing in it like a religion leads to a self-fulfilling prophecy. If we look at living nature as material nature only, it will ultimately die.

Historically there are good reasons to associate the rise of modern experimental science with a negative view of nature, emphasized in Christian theology as fallen nature.[1] With the expulsion of man from the harmonious nature of paradise, nature fell as well. Gifted with rational thinking, man's task was to bring order into this chaotic nature, to control what was called the blind forces of nature. Nature was seen as an enemy, which had to be conquered; the power of nature had to be broken. It is an attitude of distrust of nature. An experimental natural science was perfectly suited to achieve this end, taking nature as an instrument for man. The Christian theological conception of man's stewardship over nature was most of the time interpreted with this view of nature. It was anthropocentric, the rest of nature existing to serve man. It was even believed that it was man's duty to perfect nature. In his visionary book Nova Atlantis (1624), Francis Bacon, one of the founders of modern science, spoke about the transformation of one plant into another, of changing the form, the colour and behaviour of animals, of making mixtures between different species. Taking this as the Christian theological conception of man's stewardship, Lynn White (1967) became famous for his statement that Christianity allowed the exploitation the earth.[2] He was wrong,however, in generalizing this to the whole of Christian tradition. There has been another tradition, the tradition not of fallen nature, but of harmonious nature, in which nature is seen as a stable, harmonious and perfect order, which can be trusted.

The transition from the medieval concept of harmonious nature to fallen nature can be illustrated beautifully in the mining tradition. In about 1500, Paulus Niavus describes a trial against the miners, in which the miners were accused of killing Mother Earth[3]. Mother Earth appears in the trial as a woman in green dress, with a pale face, tears in her eyes, he body pierced in several places. This trial in some ways signals the end of a long medieval tradition of speaking about Mother Earth, and even about a goddess Natura. For instance, Alanus ab Insulis in Chartres describes how he had a visionary view, a meeting as he calls it himself, with Natura, the guardian of creation, the daughter of God.[4] Also with tears in her eyes, because mankind is spoiling and misusing the gifts of nature. Notice that this was at the beginning of the Fifteenth Century.

In the view of nature as harmonious, there is a positive attitude of sympathy towards nature. For those who spoke about reading in the book of nature, creation was seen as a book in which man could read the wisdom of the creator. Every creature is like a letter written by the finger of God. By looking at nature as a text, we are already one step away from the direct experience of God as being in nature. Nature is seen as God's work in the tradition of reading the book of nature, but one can still experience God. In the following centuries we see how God was austed from nature. He is outside, only coming to create nature. God becomes the watchmaker, the engineer, who created the natural mechanical laws of nature. With this, we see the beginning of a desecration of the book of nature. Galileio said that the book was written in mathematical terms. This signifies an abstract, not an empathic relation to nature. And Robert Boyle (1627-1691), the English scientist, said that the alphabet of nature was written in mechanical terms.

One of the famous scholars who spoke about reading in the book of nature was Raimundus Sabundus.[5] In 1430, he said that the Bible was given to mankind when it lost the capacity to read the book of nature. That early in history he already expressed the need for mankind to learn to read again in the book of nature. And Sabundus tells us how we have to achieve this. He says that we must take out the wisdom that is written on the body of beings, and represent it in our souls as images. We must compare one creature with the other, and combine the images, as we combine one sentence with another. And from this comparison, the true meaning will spring out . As I will show later on, what Sabundus then said, is similar to the steps of the phenomenological method, as set out by the German poet and philosopher of nature Johann von Goethe(1747-1832), who may be viewed as the founder of the phenomenological method of reading the book of nature.

Now what were the basic ideas behind this method. In the Romantic Period, around 1800 in Germany, nature is seen as visible spirit and spirit as invisible nature, to quote Friedrich von Schelling (1775-1854). The language of nature was seen as an expression of divine reason. Being an intrinsic part of nature, man in this view could let nature speak to his or her consciousness. Nature was seen as a subject, a partner, as the counterpart of ourselves. This way of thinking can be described as follows: The content of our thoughts does not come from ourselves. The more we stop talking and projecting our hypotheses upon nature, the more we learn to listen, and the more we give up the idea that nature is silent, that the birds, the winds and the waterfalls have no language, and that we are the only beings with the power of speech. Finally, knowledge of nature is not independent of knowledge of ourselves.

Perhaps we can say that time has changed, and that now nature must speak through us. We can read the book of nature because we carry the whole of nature in ourselves. Goethe taught us that we can trust our senses, that we have to develop and refine our senses and mind, rather than always putting physical instruments between ourselves and nature. The three steps of his phenomenological method can be summarized as follows:

– First we need a listening receptive attitude, and respect for creation. Trusting our senses, we have to stick to the phenomena, as directly observed. And this is what I think Sabundus meant when he said that wisdom was written on the body of beings, it was visible on the outside, in the whole organization and form.

– Secondly we need a careful perception, "caring objectivity". Surrendering to the phenomena, resigning and emptying ourselves, almost in a Taoistic sense.

– Thirdly, the images that arise need to be meditated upon. We have to develop them in our minds. And then they start revealing their secrets. It gives us qualitative knowledge, fitting ourselves into larger wholes.

The phenomenological method can thus be called a systematic method to develop experiential knowledge, of "becoming and being what is to be known".

In our culture, this phenomenological method, together with other developments, such as organic agriculture, deep ecology movement and eco-theology, possess features of the phenomenological method. The mainstream of agriculture at the moment could be called synthetic agriculture: intensive, highly specialized, industrialized. It aims more and more at closed systems, comparable to closed systems created in a scientific laboratory. Such agriculture is being removed from nature, to be controlled by man. Agriculture is segregated from nature, as we can see in a soilless horticulture, which is a perfect example of the concept of fallen nature, which has to be controlled, independent of local or regional seasonal cycles and resources. The emphasis is on technological control of pollution. It leads to increasing standardization and loss of diversity, often implying political and social engineering as well. This way of looking at nature and practising agriculture offers no outlook for renewed spiritual relations with nature.

Organic agriculture, on the other hand, is partly inspired by the phenomenological method and strives for integration. Nature is seen as a partner, as a self-regulating system, an open system, sometimes even with cosmic dimensions. Agriculture tries to attune to the developmental potentials inherent in nature. It should stimulate the productivity of the soil, instead of relying on agrochemical inputs from outside. The soil is one of the main thing to take care of. The carrying capacity of nature should not be exceeded, organic agriculture should depend on local resources. The ultimate goal is harmony between agriculture and environment. And because environments differ all over the world, so do agro-ecosystems, based on the diversity of the biosphere and on respect and responsibility for it by the local farmers. The social element weighs as heavily as the ecological element. This approach offers tremendous opportunities to develop radically new and diverse relationships with nature and to diversify its management.

The deep-ecology movement is a very good place to develop these new attitudes towards nature. This movement is inspired by the Norwegian philosopher Arne Naess, who was again much influenced by the non-violent philosophy of Mahatma Ghandi.[6] Wim Zweers, a Dutch environmental philosopher, summarizes the tenets of the deep-ecology movement, if I can speak about tenets correctly, in three points.[7]

– First, partnership, the idea that we participate as human beings in something tremendous, something great, in life in the biosphere, with an intuitive idea of the unity of all life. Keywords are connectedness and relatedness. It is based on an intense experience of nature, a great sensitivity to the richness of nature.

– Second, self-realization, through identification. Nature possesses meaning or spirituality, according to the deep-ecology movement. What is meant with self-realization is our greater Self, not our smaller ego, our greater Self which includes all that is not self-centred.

– Thirdly, biocentric egalitarianism. Respect for the intrinsic value of all life, which is the condition for identification with life. The richness and diversity of life forms are valued in themselves.

In environmental philosophy and environmental ethics, a revolution is currently taking place in the Western relation to nature. But the deep-ecology movement is not just a philosophy, it really wants to be a movement of eco-wisdom, with great economic and political consequences.

Finally let me say a few words about new developments in eco-theology. The key-word is integrity of creation, in which stewardship is more and more replaced by the idea of partnership, guardianship, believing that God is in all things, and all things are in God. Let me mention a few names. In the past many new books have been published on this subject. A little older book is by Seyyed Hossein Nasr, "Man and Nature", about the spiritual crisis of man.[8] John Cobbs book, which is about "Christian deep-ecology".[9] And James

Nash, with the book "Loving Nature, ecological integrity and Christian responsibility".[10] He pleads for a cosmocentric and biocentric view of creation, based on interdependence and relationship. He sees transcending the limits of nature as an ecological sin. He describes the cosmos as a sacred place. He combines love for nature with attitudes like receptivity, humility, and communion. In some sense, it looks like a return to the mediaeval notions of harmonious nature, to a disinterested, contemplative view of nature, of which a splendid example was Saint Francis of Assisi. The prophet, I would say, of a reverential attitude towards nature. The Saint, who speaks with the birds, and even with the four elements, with fire, water, earth and air.

I think that all these developments are examples of new ways of developing experiential knowledge. And in my opinion this kind of knowledge is and could be the basis of a real dialogue regarding agriculture and spirituality. Nasr writes "As long as theology is understood as a rational defence of the tenets of faith, there is no possibility of a real theology of nature, no way of penetrating into the inner meaning of natural phenomena and making them spiritually transparent." The dialogue should be based on inner experience, in experience we can find our friends, our brothers and sisters all over the world. Rational theology will only lead to more conflicts. Our relation to nature in our life-world has many dimensions. The scientific approach is only one of them, and an important one, but its present dominance in the universities and in society must be challenged, to create ways of systematic study of the richness of man's inner experience, in relation to nature. If we want to (re)discover the spiritual in nature, we will first have to discover it in ourselves, because the two are inseparable.

The tendencies in our culture I have mentioned, the phenomenological approach, the deep-ecology movement and eco-theology provide us with new opportunities for intercultural dialogue, because the ideals of these movements will be easily recognizable by many people from other cultures, if they are not totally westernized. For an intercultural dialogue we need the same values of openness, resignation, listening, love and respect for one another. What we need is a rebirth of nature, as it is called in the title of the latest book by Rupert Sheldrake.[11] We have forgotten nature, and here I refer to the book "Naturvergessenheit" by the German biologist and theologian, Guenther Altner.[12] And because it is unbearable to live with the idea of the "end of nature", to refer to the title of a book by McKibben, to achieve this rebirth of nature, we have to be reborn ourselves.[13]

Notes

1 The distinction between the model of "fallen nature" and the model of "harmonious nature" is taken from R.P. Sieferle: Die Krise der Menschlichen Natur. Suhrkamp, Frankfurt am Main, 1989.

2 Lynn White: The historical roots of our ecologic crisis. Svience 155 (1967) 1203-1207.

3 The trial is mentioned by Harman Boehme: Nutur und Subjekt. Suhrkamp, Frankfurt am Main, 1988.

4 Wilhelm Rath: Alanus ab Insulkis, Der Anticlaudian. Mellinger Verlag, Stuttgart, 1983.

5 Hans Boernsen: Vom Lesen im Buch der natur. Verlag am Goetheanum, Dornach (1986).

6 Arne Naess: Ecology, community and lifestyle. Cambridge University Press, Cambridge, 1991.

7 Wim Zweers: Varianten van ecologische ervaring. In: W. Achterberg & W. Zweers (ed.): Milieufilosofie, tussen theorie en praktijk. Uitgeverij Jan van Arkel, Utrecht, 1986.

8 S.H. Nasr: Man and Nature Allen & Unwin, London, 1976.

9 John B. Cobb Jr.: Sustainability: Economics, ecology and justice. Maryknoll, New York, 1992.

10 James A. Nash: Loving nature: Ecological integrity and Christian responsibility. Abingdon Press, Nashville, 1991.

11 Rupert Sheldrake: The Rebirth of Nature. The greening of the science and God. 1993,

12 Guenther Altner: Naturvergessenheit. Wissenschaftliche Buchgesellschaft. Darmstadt 1991.

13 Bill McKibben: The end of nature. Random House, New York, 1989.

CHAPTER 4

Spirituality and Agriculture

What Difference Would it Make?

Rob Witte

"There are distinctive gifts of grace, but the same Spirit, and there are distinctive ministries, yet the same Lord. There also are varieties of things acomplished, but the same God does all the energizing in them all. To each is granted the evidence of the Spirit for the common welfare. To one person is given by the Spirit a message of wisdom and to another the utterance of knowledge according to the same Spirit; to a third faith is granted by the same Spirit; to yet another the gifts of healing by the one Spirit; to another miraculous powers; to this one prophecy, to that one discrimination between spirits, to a third variety of tongues, and to yet another the ability to interpret tongues. All these abilities one and the same Spirit energizes, distributing to each individual exactly as He pleases." (1 Corinthians 12:1-11)

Challenge of an Intercultural Encounter

As one of the organizers, I had high expectations of an inter(agri)cultural dialogue on agriculture and spirituality. At the end of the day, I was both inspired and puzzled. Inspired, because so many people had shown interest in the topic. Apparently they were looking for some sort of mutual support in finding their way and defining their position in the relationship God-man-nature. Puzzled too, because it appeared to be so difficult to express inner motivations or experiences in such a way, that others (often from a different cultural background) could still understand it.

My own enthusiasm for the idea of an intercultural dialogue on issues like faith and inspiration, beliefs and values, is based on my work as an expatriate in the Philippines. There I had encountered fascinating world views, which opened new perspectives on my own position in the cosmos. The Chinese philosophy underlying acupuncture confronted me with "energies" in my own body. The local farmers' perceptions of the influence of the moon on agricultural crops confronted me with the probability of cosmic influences on our earthly existence. Both inner functioning and outer influences beyond the mere physiscal or chemical causes appeared plausible.

This new perspective puzzled me a lot, since I could not grasp the underlying world views or life-philosophies. For example, the yin and yang dichotomy of the Chinese world view has a lot of connotations, which I only understood later: Yang corresponds with sun, strong, male, conquering, extrovert, bright; yin corresponds with moon, weak, female, obeying, introvert, bleak. Neither could I judge to what extent these views were mere beliefs without any scientific basis. And if so, were they then less valuable than my own? And how should I judge these views, if they were based on ages of observations of phenomena, which had until then simply escaped my attention as well as "western" scientific scrutiny? Doesn't that open new perpectives for research and practice?

Another question still at the back of my mind, is concerned with the value system and morality of such a different culture. More implicit than explicit it contains ethical "codes" that are strange and sometimes uncomfortable. Do such values enrich explicit or implicit values in my own culture? Or are they diametrically opposed and at conflict, and therefore so perhaps even unacceptable? A good example for such a conflict in ethics was the common practice in the Philippines to slaughter dog as an ingredient for festive meals, or as a snack accompanying a drinking session. Under the former Marcos dictatorship, this custom was forbidden, under pressure of the English government. But is killing a dog for food more savage than killing a pig or a chicken?

By participating in the organization of the symposium, I hoped to get a better insight into this sort of issues, so far as they were related to agriculture, which is my professional interest. In the remainder of this article I want to recall some of the issues, which cropped up in the speeches and workshops of the symposium together with my own comments. I hope that my effort of summarizing some of the main issues of the symposium can be used to develop an agenda for a continuing inter(agri)cultural dialogue on agriculture and spirituality.

Spirituality

Looking back at the papers, the speeches and the workshops of the symposium, it is remarkable that no short, clear and comprehensive description of

the term "spirituality" was given. Numerous components of a spiritual attitude were mentioned and discussed. Many related issues, like religion, belief,
beliefs, cosmology were mentioned. The question was raised explicitly as the
first item for discussion in the six workshops: "What would we call spirituality?" But a working definition still has to be formulated. I will mention
"ingredients" which have been put into words in the symposium.

In the invitation to the symposium, two issues about spirituality were
mentioned:

1. the relationship God-man-nature;

2. the limitations of an objectifying attitude towards nature and agriculture,
which becomes apparent in an acute ecological crisis.

Huizer concentrates on the spirituality he has encountered in his meeting
with other people. Resigning from developmental intervention, he participated in Third World people's struggles for survival and justice. They then
allowed and stimulated him "to share all their frequent spiritual traditional
celebrations about life and survival, and particularly death, that appeared to
help them much to remain cheerful and resistant under rather desperate conditions of (rather covert) struggle". From various historical and cultural contexts, Huizer mentions some elements of spirituality, which he called "experiential knowledge" (i.e. knowledge by experience):

– spiritual healing, herbal medicine, acupuncture;

– guarding and protecting spirits for tribal territories, which guide many
aspects of daily life in order to keep harmony with the natural environment;

– a holistic religious awareness of the unity and continuity of life and after-
life, good and evil, natural and supernatural;

– an unspoken conviction that a juster and more egalitarian society should
be reached;

– "knowledge of the Inmost Nature of beings" (quoted from Tempels, 1959).

Shiva explains the Indian view on the relationship God-man-nature with
the connotations of the word precriti: it is the word for nature in most languages, derived from Sanscrit, in which it means the original activating force.
But it is also the word for creativity. It is the inner drive, the inward growth of
every aspect of life, in all its diversity. In Indian cosmology, the divine is
nature, and self-organization is seen as built into life itself. It is the very definition of life. Respect for that self-organization is what divinity is about.

Verhoog concentrates on the attitude needed to experience the spiritual in
nature, which he characterizes as the phenomenological method and as "read-

ing the book of nature", in which man can see the wisdom of the creator, God. The elements of this method are in short:

1. a listening, receptive and respectful attitude;
2. a caring and resigning objectivity, emptying ourselves to surrender to the phenomena observed;
3. meditating on the images that come up, in order for them to reveal their true meaning.

Verhoog invites us to find ways of systematically studying the richness of man's inner experience: "If we want to (re)discover the spiritual in nature, we will first have to discover it in ourselves, because the two are inseparable."

Workshop participants mentioned various aspects of spirituality, which I have tried to systematize a little:

For many participants, spirituality is a sense of relatedness and connectedness. They express such connectedness either in all-encompassing terms, such as creation, nature, even the stars, or in concrete elements such as land, soil, plants and livestock, and other people. Other participants describe spirituality more in terms of attitude and ethics: care, sharing, equality, modesty and respect. Still others can be brought together under the term "experiencing" to cover their ideas regarding spirituality: They experienced security, beauty, or the presence of God. Also the sense of belonging, which was called relatedness and connectedness should be called a spiritual experience.

When rereading our invitation for the symposium, it struck me that we, as organizers of the symposium, focused mainly on the spirituality in relation to nature. Verhoog adds to this the need to rediscover the spiritual in ourselves, whereas Huizer adds the dimension of spirituality in relation to others, in social struggles for justice.

Spirituality and Morality

Many of the issues mentioned in relation to spirituality will not be accepted as signs of the presence of the divine by Christian theologians, who would rather call them superstition. The fundamental difference in cosmology between Christians, Muslims and Jews and other religions is expressed well by Shiva. The monotheistic religions will maintain that God, as subject, as Creator, made heaven and earth. While other religions see nature as Divine. Frans Verkleij, in this volume, also refers to this controversy in Christian theology, using the terminology of "transcendence" versus "immanence".

Both Verkleij and Verhoog reach back to historic mediaeval world views to trace roots of a Christian theology that was more friendly towards nature. In this context, I want to refer to Saint Francis of Assisi (1182-1226), by translating some fragments by the Franciscan priest Rotzetter (1981). "Francis included the animals and all other creatures in his mission, e.g. by preaching to the birds. He takes the missionary command of Marc 16 quite literally: "Go into the whole world and preach the gospel to every creature." After preaching to the birds, he bitterly reproached himself that he did not think of preaching to the speechless creatures before....He maintains a relationship of dialogue with every creature. In every thing and animal, he recognized a personal dignity; he called them brother and sister. Towards the end of his life this attitude was transformed into a poem, the Hymn of the Sun, which sings about everything: heaven and earth, which is the universe, air, water, soil and fire, the elements of which everything was made in the ancient worldview. It was Francis' conviction that God is everything in everyone, which makes every thing or animal – and of course everybody – indispensible." This attitude of Francis shows that we can be respectful and compassionate to other creatures, even if we do not accept them as "divine".

If I reconsider the various forms of spirituality of the Bantu (Huizer), the peoples of India (Shiva), or the respectful attitude towards nature which forms the basis of ecological agriculture (Verhoog), the connection between them is the inner knowledge of the true nature of creatures, and the conviction that these all have an inherent value which should be respected. This respect for the "Inmost Nature" of things, plants, animals and people forces us to take a stand on values, morality, good and evil. Once we have recognized that other creatures have a value of their own, we have to decide ourselves whether what we are planning to do with such a creature is right or wrong. This is where spirituality and morality meet: in our everyday decisions.

Agriculture and Spirituality

The relation between agriculture and spirituality is a tricky one. The most poignant statements, recorded in the symposium workshops, illustrate this: "Spirituality is the celebration of life. But we are killing so much in agriculture." At the other end of the spectrum of participants' views, one person said, "Talking about spirituality seems a little contradictory, because there are a lot of hungry people," and another said, "Talking about spirituality or organic agriculture is not the point. We have to feed the world." Both these views express concern about matters of life and death. The first one by expressing concern for non-human life, which is sacrificed for the sake of agricultural productivity. The latter two participants express concern for the human lives, which are at stake if agricultural productivity is not high enough or agricultural produce is not distributed well, resulting in malnutrition, undernourishment, hunger and even death.

These views are extremes of an unavoidable contradiction in any discussion on agriculture and ethics. In order to survive, man has to interfere in nature, deciding on life and death for other creatures.

If agricultural productivity is the only focus, issues like nature conservation, pollution, animal welfare and the intrinsic values of other creatures are easily sacrificed. But if ethical, aesthetical (or spiritual?) issues become central, it is easy to forget that agriculture is producing the food, on which our very survival depends. Still I think that one cannot simply escape from this contradiction by referring to hunger or food scarcity. At present, world agriculture can produce enough food to feed the world, and hunger and starvation should be seen as a problem of income distribution, or as a poverty problem, rather than as a result of food shortages. Acute food shortage at present mostly results from disasters, wars and such like.

Locally, farmers often have to cope individually with the consequences of (worldwide) agribusiness developments. Some of the statements of workshop participants show that practising a different agriculture individually has severe consequences for the economic viability of that farmer under present economic and political conditions.

As a Dutch participant in the workshops stated, "My father did not want to intensify livestock keeping, he wanted to treat his animals with respect. But as a consequence, the sons of his neighbours still can continue their fathers' farms, while my father's farm has inadequate economic prospects for me to continue it. Political and economic structures prohibit a different practice of farming." Another participant told the story of a farming family who decided to move to a farm in the new agricultural lands of the Dutch North-East Polder. By that step, they decided to follow the conventional wisdom of agricultural policy and extension. "From that moment on, they were pushed around by the bank, they no longer got a moment's rest." And a third participant, an extension worker from Ethiopia, told, "I tried to convince our farmers to use chemical fertilizers, but they did not want it. They wanted to use the materials from their own land only. Now I see that I was wrong, but these were the scientific Western things we had learned at school." "Governments have various ways of forcing people to accept new technologies, and then there is often a conflict between government extension workers, who want to introduce that technology, and local farmers, who want to keep their own traditions. These extension workers are not free in what to tell to their clients."

These examples and experiences show that it is difficult to escape from main-stream developments in agriculture towards a more spiritual attitude.

Spirituality and Science

Verhoog touched upon a different matter of life and death: "If we look at living nature as material only, it will ultimately die". In this respect, both Verhoog and Shiva argue that Western civilization is reaching a dead end, by ignoring the life dimension of nature, agriculture and human existence. It is interesting to note that Verhoog cautiously limited his criticism to "the experimental method of modern natural science", and the negative view of nature as "fallen nature", which considers nature as an enemy to be used, conquered and controlled. Shiva, on the other hand, contended that Western science and the mechanistic cosmology it has developed have themselves become a religion, comparing scientists with priests, whom you have to believe in. If we take this line of reasoning somewhat further, should we call scientists who "believe in the materialistic assumptions as if it were a religion" as prophets and priests of death? Such rhetoric might work out well, as an eye-opener for people who believe that scientific proof should prevail over moral, religious or ethical values. But as an opening bid for an intercultural dialogue between holistic tendencies and reductionist sciences, such an exaggeration might be obstructive rather than fruitful.

So what then are the issues for serious reflection, where do the guests of our symposium mention problems or prospects for spirituality in relation (or confrontation) with science? The most basic dilemma has been expressed by Verhoog, where he stated, "It is often forgotten that the experimental method of modern natural science can neither deny nor confirm the existence of a spiritual world. It deliberately limits itself to what can be tested with experimental methods." As long as the sciences do not want to discuss observations based on a more empathic methodology, or as long as the more holistic approaches do not produce results that can also be tested experimentally, there may be no basis at all for a dialogue, since both sides apparently do not appreciate each others contribution as valid.

Huizer referred to spirituality as an inherent part of indigenous "experiential knowledge" in the context of the daily struggle for survival. He illustrates that Western social researchers biassed to the middle-class could not detect the power relations involved in "development" projects. So neither could they explain the logic of the resistance by peasants or indigenous peoples to development projects. Huizer pointed out that the persistance of such resistance can often be traced back to its spiritual components. As a perspective for dialogue, he apparently wanted to combine the holistic, caring and redistributive aspirations of environmental and popular resistance movements with a participatory scientific approach. However, he wanted Western scientists interested in such efforts to be aware of possible uses of their insights by the power elites.

In her speech, Shiva criticized the sciences in two ways. First she referred to the British Imperial plant scientists just after World War II, who started to promote DDT and other insecticides even though there were hardly any pests to speak of. Secondly, Shiva pointed to manipulative and monopolizing consequences of the most recent developments in the biotechnological and the legal field. The development of a technology that allows translocation of bits of DNA across species barriers reinforces an instrumental approach by the bio-technological sciences, which sees plants or animals just as bioreactors. In combination with the extension of patents to genetically modified life-forms and the inclusion of such intellectual property rights in GATT, this has given investors in biotechnology enormous power. At this moment, the biological consequences of these genetical manipulations, as well as the resulting concentration of economic power can hardly be foreseen.

Rightly Shiva argues that biotechnological issues like genetic engineering in plants and animals provide explosive material for an intercultural dialogue on spirituality and agriculture, as these issues show the consequences of a manipulative and "value-free" science in the extreme.

Problems and Prospects for a Dialogue

In the workshops, participants reflected on the issues "What difference would spirituality make for the practice of agriculture" and "What tension between "spirituality" and "agriculture" do you experience."

If I may try to formulate a general line, based on many observations by participants, I see two main issues: "respect" and "balance".

Respect for the vital and behavioral needs of animals, respect for the culture and world view of farmers with whom extension workers, development workers and researchers are working. Respect for nature and creation in it's own right. Or should I say, respect for the divine spark that we may recognize in any aspect of life?

Balance between inner and outer, or feminine and masculine. Aspects of the inner life which were mentioned in this sense were: convictions, emotions, ethics. With the outer life, aspects like learning, scientific knowledge, technological and economic developments, the material things were associated.

The issue of spirituality is not the easiest one to start an inter-cultural dialogue on. Spirituality touches the core of deeply felt emotional, religious and motivational layers in our minds and souls. The feeling of being understood by someone else in this respect may cause great joy, being misunderstood, on the other hand, is very painful.

In this sense, as organizers of a symposium on such an issue, we took a great risk, and in the workshops some of these risks became hard reality. It is difficult to express deeply felt beliefs or emotions in another language than your mother tongue. It is threatening to express deep concerns in a group where you hardly know any of the other participants, and the more so if the organization of such a workshop almost forces you to say at least something. And if you had expected a serious response or question in answer to your opening statement, you may have found out that time was lacking for a deeper discussion.

One participant expressed his anxiety rather clearly: "I think this group is too big to handle such sensitive issues." Others avoided sharing the more personal experiences or views, and instead started to talk about articles or books they had read, or stories they had heard. This clearly illustrates the point made by Henk Verhoog: "To have a good intercultural dialogue with other people we need (the same values of) openness, resignation, listening, love and respect for the other."

As to the aim of such a dialogue, we have to be clear about our motives: a dialogue is not a discussion in the sense that a majority decision or even a consensus has to be reached. Any open or covert effort of trying to convince or persuade the other participants to your own view or vision must be treated with suspicion. I see a dialogue rather as an effort to further understanding between people and peoples. Trying to reach such an understanding is in the first place an enriching, and therefore may be already a spiritual experience.

CHAPTER 5

Spirituality and Ecological Agriculture

Frans Verkleij

Agriculture in the Netherlands is in crisis. It produces too much and places too heavy a burden on the environment. It respects the intrinsic value of domestic animals too little. The confidence that technology will solve these problems in the near future may not be justified. My thesis is that these problems cannot be separated from agriculture's conception of its main task, the production of food. In this article I will juxtapose this conception, typical of industrial agriculture, against another conception, that of ecological agriculture. Then I will examine these conceptions from a theological point of view. Finally I will argue that spirituality should find a new place in agriculture.

Industrial Agriculture: Man opposed to Nature

Agriculture is the domain of the earth, mankind, plants and animals. So food production is fundamentally different from production of non-living products like cars or radios. The process of increase in scale and intensification increases efficiency in the industrial production of goods, but goes astray in the production of food. Examples can easily be given, showing that increase in scale and intensification have ended in disaster. The "Dust Bowl" in the US in the third decade of this century, when huge areas of arable land fell prey to the wind as a consequence of erosion through mismanagement, is an illustration that even then the industrial approach to agriculture went astray. Intensive animal husbandry in the Netherlands illustrates that the industrial approach to food production (bio-industry) does not work. Despite tight hygienic measures, epidemics arise regularly, and then require severe counter-measures, such as the slaughter of all animals. Intensive growth of potatoes, with large areas under one cultivar, can only be protected with great effort against diseases like *Phythophthora;* in favourable conditions (humid and warm) a small focus of infection can destroy the whole crop in a short time. In greenhouse horticulture, production of crops like tomato and cucumber is approached like an industry, and has run into problems in recent years because of overproduction and competition from countries around the Mediterranean and changing opinions of consumers who dislike tomatoes produced in an industrial way.

The underlying conception of the industrial approach to agriculture is anthropocentrism, that postulates that human beings exploit may and manipulate nature as they wish. Biotechnology, which provides the means to break bariers between species, takes this conception for granted. This conception also arises from fear and distrust of nature, which is seen as an opponent who must be conquered in order to prevent mankind from being conquered by nature.

This conception could be explained theologically in two ways. First, it fits into a theology that opposes natural theology. The latter has the view that knowledge of God can be deduced from our knowledge of the world, since God and mankind (creation) have features in common. In the theology that rejects natural theology, most sharply formulated by Karl Barth, knowledge of God can never be deduced from knowledge of nature. God is "der ganz Andere" (the Completely Different); God shows himself only by Revelation (mainly Scriptures). The danger inherent in this theology is that the notion that God cannot be known in nature turns into a distrust of nature.

Second, this conception has always been grounded in the interpretation of Genesis 1: 26-28, where God created man in his own image and likeness, in order that "man should have dominion over the fish in the sea, …and over every living thing that moves on the earth". White (1967) was one of the first to indicate that Christianity has legitimated the submission of nature by mankind from this divine commission with disastrous consequences. The *"dominium terrae"* is deeply anchored in Christian tradition.

White's thesis has been widely discussed. One of the conclusions of this discussion has been that besides the tradition of *"dominium terrae"*, there is also a tradition of stewardship. In the latter tradition, the commission to mankind is not to subdue nature, but to minister it, in order that future generations can enjoy its fruits.

Ecological Agriculture: Mankind in Partnership with Nature

In ecological agriculture, mankind does not oppose nature, but tries to co-operate as much as possible. By stimulating ecological processes in nature, problems typical of industrial agriculture show up much less frequently. Let me give some examples.

Soil fertility is not maintained by external inputs of synthetic manure, but by placing leguminous crops in rotation. These are able to fix nitrogen from the air in a form available to the plant. Moreover, manure from cattle on the mixed farm is spread on the land to maintain fertility. Manure is not a waste product but an essential to balanced farm management. As a consequence, upper limits of nitrate in surface water are seldom exceeded in this type of agriculture, in contrast to what happens in industrial agriculture. Essential nutrients like phosphate and trace elements that are not present in the soil in an available form for the plant are made available in ecological agriculture by stimulating the activity of micro-organisms in the soil. Pests and diseases are seldom a problem because of the use of several cropping measures. For example, soil-borne diseases seldom occur because of a wide crop rotation; many pests and diseases are controlled by natural enemies. Excesses that would occur in bio-industrial approaches are avoided, and the intrinsic value of animals is respected as much as possible.

In ecological agriculture, too, mankind is acknowledged as the centre of nature. The farmer steers production in the direction he desires. However, this control is based upon ecological processes and remains within the carrying capacity of the agro-ecosystem. Agriculture is always culture *(cultura)*: nature is transformed by the farmer. Thus, in ecological agriculture, too, man stands above nature. But this position of power is handled in a moral way.

Imago Dei

In Mediaeval theology, God was felt to be present in his creation, in humans as well as in all other creatures. Thomas Aquinas mentioned *vestigia dei* (vestiges of God in all creatures) and *imago dei* (image of God in mankind). God's immanence in all creatures implies solidarity between man and other creatures. At the end of the Middle Ages, the notion of a bond between Creator and creature became more and more fragile until William Ockham finally denied such a bond. Man stood alone in creation. As a consequence of this development, God's transcedence was increasingly emphasized at the expense of his immanence. The confidence that the world is, in essence, good disappeared. This development made way for man's emancipation. However the reverse of this process is becoming increasingly clear in our time.

The Mediaeval conceptions seem far from our secular society. Nevertheless, let me argue that those conceptions need to be remodelled in order to revive the notion of the bond between God and creation. This revived notion implies that solidarity between man and nature gains a new basis. Moltmann (1985) tried to give a new content to the concept of *imago dei.* Man is linked to the other creatures by evolution (man has developed from other creatures) and by ecology (man shares with other creatures the same fragile earth). Moltmann uses the term *"imago mundi"* (image of the world) for the bond. Man is a micro-cosmos, in which he represents all creatures (the world) for God, realizing that he cannot exist without the other creatures and cannot understand himself without them. As *imago dei* (the only creature created in the image of God), he represents God in the community of creatures and fulfils God's will (Moltmann 1985, p. 193-197).

Spirituality

Let me elaborate on the conception of *imago dei,* that one should co-operate with nature instead of subduing it, in the daily practice of agriculture. Here I want to introduce the term spirituality. Spirituality implies concern for God, expressing God's presence. The spiritual exists within as well as besides the material. A materialistic attitude denies the existence of the spiritual besides the material. If we assume a more spiritual attitude to nature, then we acknowledge that nature is ultimately from God ("The earth is the Lord's, and all its fullness", Psalm 24:1), and is not freely at our disposal.

What is a spiritual attitude to nature? It encompasses respect, amazement and modesty (Achterhuis, 1992, p. 30). Respect for the intrinsic value of plant and animal, that we may not put aside but must appreciate. Only with respect we may use plant or animal. Amazement for the ingenious way in which the processes of life proceed; "as the mustard seed, the least of all seeds, but when it is grown is greater than the herbs and becomes a tree, so that the birds of the air come and nest in its branches" (Mt 13: 31). Modesty stems from the notion that we are dependent on other creatures and cannot live without them.

In Christianity, there is room for such a spirituality. Saint Francis of Assisi is the striking example. Feminine theology acknowledges the involvement of mankind in the earth. Non-Western religious sources also give leads for such a spirituality.

Spirituality is not only a spiritual attitude, but expresses itself in doing. In ancient times, agriculture was an area in which spirituality was self-evident, because food production was the basis of life. Witness to this is the metaphore of mother earth (Gaia), portrayed in many myths. Harvest festivals (Thanksgiving Day) remind us of this spiritual bond. An ecological agriculture, in which the earth, plants and animals are approached with respect, amazament and modesty provides the frame for a new spirituality.

Literature

Achterhuis, H.J. (1990). *Van moeder aarde tot ruimteschip: humanisme en milieucrisis,* Inaugural lecture, Agricultural University Wageningen (NL).
Moltmann, J. (1985). *Gott in der Schpöfung, Ökologische Schöpfungslehre,* Kaiser, Munich.
White, L. (1967). The historical roots of our ecological crisis, *Science,* 155: 1203-1207.

CHAPTER 6

Ecological Spirituality as Point of Departure for an Intercultural Dialogue

Wim Zweers

Development cooperation is increasingly coming under attack. This is due to a variety of reasons, including no doubt the limited effectiveness of numerous development projects, particularly if initiated by governments or multilateral organizations such as the World Bank. This too has a variety of reasons, but according to many, including people from the development scene itself, the assumption at least seems justified that this has something to do with the neglect of the so-called "cultural factor"[1].

It seems so obvious that this cultural factor should be taken into account when passing on, or sharing, knowledge and skills in certain sectors. However, there is little evidence of this being the case, or if it is, it is all too seldom put into practice[2]. After all, it involves a lot of things, and in the following I will try to clarify this within the context of intercultural dialogue. I will first discuss *world views*: what does it mean (for us, Westerners) to take account of another (culture's) world view, and to what extent does this require a basis for common understanding? Secondly I will explore the possible form and role of spiritual solidarity with nature, i. e. *ecological spirituality* in this context, and in particular the form this could take, if this is to be of any benefit for an intercultural dialogue, from a Western point of view. Finally, even if ecological spirituality were a good point of departure for such a dialogue, that in itself is insufficient to create a model of action in the relations between

---

1 Cf. Jan Pronk (Dutch Minister for Development Cooperation), *De kritische grens; Beschouwingen over tweespalt en orde*, Prometheus, Amsterdam, 1994, p. 187.
2 As for example by Bertus Haverkort and David Millar, who want to create a "synergetic cooperation" between "participatory technology development" and "indigenous cosmology", using the idea that "Western science could learn from (in this case, wz) the Talensis" (a tribe in Ghana) as a starting point. See their "Farmer's experiments and cosmovision" in: *ILEIA Newsletter for Low External Input and Sustainable Agriculture*, vol. 8,1992 no. 1, p. 26-28. However, I gather that something of this sort will not be met with wide approval among development workers.

Western and non-Western countries. For that purpose, this spirituality should be considered as an (experiential) component of a more broadly conceived "participatory attitude towards nature". This requires a discussion of *basic attitudes towards nature* in more general terms, and the possibly practical significance of such an approach. The last point applies, among others, to the field of agriculture, which is well illustrated by Kockelkorens's report on genetic manipulation of plants (elsewhere in this volume).

A View on World Wiews

A first condition for an intercultural dialogue – though one which is very difficult for Westerners with their universalistic conception of knowledge – is to take non-Western cultures fully *seriously*. This might seem almost ridiculously self-evident, but is not so. For instance, when talking about "holy places", one should not think: that's just what those people believe but in reality it's nonsense of course. Instead one should accept it as a realistic possibility operating for them there and then, just as *our* conceptions of reality (metaphysics) or ourselves (anthropology) operate for us in our time and place – at least, that's what many people say.

Whoever wants to leave *science* out of consideration here is underestimating the relevance of the presuppositions determining and restricting it. No science whatsoever can go beyond its own metaphysical limitations, and neither can the modern-empirical variety. Modern science does not so much deny this in theory, but does categorically deny its practical relevance, namely through its pretension of universalizability, saying not only: "this applies to everyone, independent of time and place", but also: "something different *cannot* apply and so must be rejected". However, any science is accompanied by its own metaphysics, and an immanent metaphysics – limited by the bonds of human-ness – which "tolerates no other gods in its presence" is not metaphysics but a narrow-minded mistake. The point is not that modern science or its concomitant mechanistic-dualistic metaphysics cannot be applied equally well elsewhere (in certain areas at least); rather, the point is that – and with no less metaphysical, philosophical-anthropological and epistemological importance – different perspectives can have their own validity too: we can accept them "for them" perhaps, but – and that actually is the key question here – can we accept them "for us" as well?

Huizer (in his contribution to this volume) wonders whether Westerners really can understand indigenous knowledge systems without "…transcending the paradigmatic limitations of the Western scientific world view common since Francis Bacon". I would answer: no, that is not possible, if only because that particular world view *denies* that something else could be true. That is what I mean by "not taking seriously". Huizer also refers to the fascinating example of alchemy as analysed by Morris Berman. This is something from our own culture, though far distant in time. Did alchemy really work (as some historical reports say) or was it only an unsuccessful early phase of modern chemistry (setting aside the depth-psychological aspect revealed by Jung and others)? However, Berman's rather bewildering answer is that we cannot know what the alchemist did "in reality", because "in reality" means what the alchemist did, and not what we modern people (could) do[3]. The idea that – in this case – there might be something like an "in reality" other than the alchemist's practice, and that we, through modern science, could have access to it and were able to say whether it was nonsense or not, expresses the locked-up nature of a scientific world view which does not acknowledge its own metaphysical limitations and is thus, from the very start, unable to live up to its own pretension of universalizability. Whatever could be universalizable, *this* certainly is not. This is what intercultural dialogue is about, a dialogue which is in some ways comparable to an historical dialogue: alchemy is an instructive parable whem we look at something like animism, and we can recognize some aspects of non-Western cultures in our own Renaissance.

It is necessary, therefore, to relativize one's own world view or metaphysics. However, one doesn't have to do this "for oneself": any lack of engagement in *this* respect would be altogether wrong here, a deconstructivist-postmodernist error of use to nobody, either ourselves or non-Westerners. We do do it, though, "for others": there are many, culturally very different "paths towards reality", and I cannot see that one would be preferable to any other, except when seen from one's own perspective. Using our own perspective is exactly what we do for ourselves, but what we almost by definition cannot for this reason do for others. This can be described simply as mutual tolerance. That means respecting the value of the other: not *our* value but *his* own value, his *intrinsic value*. Everyday experience shows, however, that that alone is far from easy. Nevertheless, I am looking for something that goes further than tolerance only. Tolerance alone means that one remains (personally) unin-

---

3   Morris Berman, *The Reenchantment of the World*, Cornell Univ. Press, Ithaca, 1981, p. 91vv.

volved, and that is what I – though as an outsider in this field – think I come across in some (cultural-)anthropological *descriptions* of non-Western knowledge systems: while showing great respect for what is different, it is not looked at as being intended or even relevant for *myself.* A true dialogue requires something more than this.

I would like to defend the thesis that something of this sort – that we would also be able to understand *from within* some part of that other culture – could be possible (if at all) with regard to or on the basis of a fundamental solidarity with nature. However, if we are to understand something of that sort in other cultures, we too should have something similar at our disposal: after all, we never can understand someone else's world view if we do not have a world view of our own. Not only in the "formal" sense mentioned above[4]: the realization that one's own conviction is "simply" a conviction, and not a universally valid scientific truth. Moreover, there has to be some sort of elementary content-oriented, normative agreement, some recognition in that other culture of what we too could be concerned about in our relationship with nature (see also Verhoog's contribution on this topic).

This is not the right place to discuss in depth the existence and character of this fundamental solidarity with nature in many non-Western cultures; it is also not within my competence. That discussion has been taken up by Shiva and Huizer in this volume, and in particular Shiva's warning against formulating (too) global theories about complex cultures characterized by much diversity is of particular importance. But even Shiva purports that despite the diversity of Indian cosmology, there still is a common denominator: an awareness that nature is divine. The divine does not create nature as an outside entity, it *is* nature. Moreover it is nature seen as a coherent unity, and not as a collection of separate pieces which can be manipulated by humanity at will (as is so characteristic for much of Western metaphysics). Citing the missionary Tempels on Africa, Huizer too emphasizes, despite all the differences which we should by no means underestimate, this essential aspect of "...recognizing a unity in the order of beings in the universe", an order encompassing the spiritual world, originating from God and so to be respected.

This attention to spirituality can be found in a very different way in non-

---

4   Cf. the discussion on democracy as a formal-procedural concept as against a more content-oriented and normative notion. Without detracting from the importance of the procedural aspect (e. g. to guarantee equality in a dialogue or equal contribution in a decision-making process), in the first place it will have to be *about* something too.

Western environmental and development organizations, which sometimes clearly point to the necessity of having a spiritual component in the theory and practice of a policy aimed at sustainability. A memorandum formulated by Asian Non Governmental Organizations[5] cites the growing alienation from the spiritual bonds with nature and with the (local) community as one of the causes of the failure of development cooperation and of the increasing gap between poor and rich countries. It is necessary to make a conscious choice for a different policy to restore (among others) these bonds: this is not only for purposes of survival, but also as a possible step towards a next phase in the evolution of life itself.

Essential for such an alternative is "that most fundamental of all spiritual insights, i. e. that life is an expression of a single spiritual unity and that the spiritual growth of the individual consists of advancement towards the full, conscious realization of this unity. Spirituality, community and a bonding to place or habitat are central values that have unified the Asian cultures over centuries." This does not mean that technology has to be rejected, or that we return to a premodern way of life: on the contrary, we should look for "new levels of social, intellectual and spiritual advancement far beyond the reach of past generations", levels that are now coming within our grasp "because of the current potential to melt both ancient and modern wisdom to this end".

Obviously, this memorandum pays relatively a lot of attention to the institutional side of the matter: a new economic together with a new social and political practice. While a different economic practice cannot in itself restore a lost sense of spiritual solidarity, a reversal of the dynamics of alienation, so deeply rooted in present economic thought, can be "an important step toward enabling people to rediscover the spiritual core of their lives and its connection to community and nature". "The political awakening provides an energizing force for change. The spiritual awakening gives direction to this force".

This memorandum, then, gives us a *general* view, broadening the importance of spiritual solidarity with nature in India and Africa – accentuated by Shiva and Huizer – to something which is equally important for Western cul-

---

5   *Economy, Ecology and Spirituality; Toward a Theory and Practice of Sustainability*, The Asian NGO Coalition (Manila), IRED Asia (Colombo), The People-Centered Development Forum (New-York), August 1993, esp. p. 6-8, 12, 14. This memorandum will be published in the Netherlands in 1995 by Aktie Strohalm, Utrecht.

tures[6], and this with good reason. I noted earlier that from the viewpoint of tolerance we should respect non-Western world views since they work apparently for them, just as we view our (mechanistic-materialistic-dualistic) world view as working for us. The latter, however, is becoming more and more doubtful: many people find the fundamental character of the environmental and nature crisis conclusive proof that our Western world view is *not* working for us, and that the time has come to look for something completely different. To take other cultures seriously is therefore not only a matter of tolerance and respect, it is also of vital concern for ourselves. In this way a very different perspective on the intercultural dialogue emerges: that it is precisely in this fundamental solidarity with nature that we could *learn* something from "developing countries".

This by no means implies that non-Western countries should be idealized; doubtlessly we would find many aspects of life there unacceptable, including in respect to nature and the environment. Nor does it imply that we should not develop in our own way alternatives for the modern world view (including a transformed – less reductionistic and monopolistic – concept of science and rationality). We can no more adopt something from other cultures, than they can from us (cf. the failure of many development projects). However, we can listen to the "tale of man, nature and God" in other cultures, and we can be inspired and motivated by it in our own search for an alternative. We need to complete the whole "triangle of meaning" of man, nature and God, which traditionally in the Western world are also the three basic possible orientations of meaning. In this sense, since the beginning of the modern era, rather we too still belong to the developing countries. Needless to say our effectiveness in development cooperation can only be enhanced by recognizing this (and by an actual endeavour to do something about it in our own way).

Ecological Spirituality

I will now explain briefly my understanding of ecological spirituality, as a possible specifically Western approach to the experience of a fundamental solidarity with nature, and so perhaps as a possible basis for an intercultur-

---

6   However, such a view is rarely met in Western environmental and development organizations: in the Netherlands Aktie Strohalm is one of the few exceptions perhaps.

al dialogue. After a general description I will discuss two related aspects: scientific and theological[7].

The shortest possible description of ecological spirituality is: experience of a meaningful solidarity with a nature which has intrinsic valuable quality. Solidarity with natural reality on the level of meaning, i. e. as something which is co-constitutive for our humanity, must be experienced or lived through: it is not only knowledge but also inner experience of belonging to the great whole we call "nature", in its widest sense. Ecological spirituality, interpreted in this way, is in the first instance an immanent or "horizontal" spirituality. It is directed towards the world around us, but not a world consisting only of humans: it is a world of animals, plants, things, and humans too, as well as the ecosystems into which they organize themselves, up to and including the earth as a whole: "Gaia". That is a world which, in all its complexity and inherent purposiveness, is unimaginable and awe-inspiring, both in space (ecosystems) and time (evolutionary development).

The following quotes, from an ecologist, a philosopher and a nature conservationst[8], may give more insight into this feeling of solidarity. First the ecologist, Paul Shepard: "Ecological thinking... requires a kind of vision across boundaries. The epidermis of the skin is ecologically like a pond surface or a forest soil, not a shell so much as a delicate interpenetration. It reveals the self ennobled and extended..., as a part of the landscape and the ecosystem". That is the viewpoint of an ecologist, a philosophically inspired ecologist, with much influence on all those who take ecology not only as an empirical science but also as an ideological or metaphysical perspective.

The philosopher is Holmes Rolston, one of the best known and, in my opinion, most original environmental philosophers of our time. Rolston, sitting beside a little lake, observes: "Does not my skin resemble this lake surface? Neither lake nor self has independent being...Inlet waters of North Inlet (the name of the lake, wz) are part of my circulatory system; and the more lit-

---

7   On ecological spirituality see further my *Participeren aan de natuur: Ontwerp voor een ecologisering van het wereldbeeld*, Uitgeverij Jan van Arkel, Utrecht, 1995, p. 394-457 (on theology esp. p. 442-457), as well as p. 301-345 and p. 467-479 (on science).

8   See respectively: P. Shepard, Ecology and Man: a Viewpoint, in: R. Disch (Ed.), *The Ecological Conscience*, Englewood Cliffs 1970, p. 57; H. Rolston, Lake Solitude: the Individual in Wildness, in his *Philosophy Gone Wild; Essays in Environmental Ethics*, New-York 1986, p. 224; J. Seed, Anthropocentrism, Appendix E, in: B. Devall and G. Sessions, *Deep Ecology, living as if nature mattered*, Salt Lake City 1985, p. 243.

erally we take this truth the more nearly we understand it". He clearly takes the idea beyond the metaphor: we will have to take it to be "real" (or, for that matter, "serious"), or we will not be able to understand it at all. The reality-constituting dimension of metaphors is more appropriate here than their reductionistic interpretation.

Finally John Seed, an Australian nature conservationist, who has dedicated himself to the preservation of the Queensland rainforest, and who is one of the foremost proponents of encouraging the experience-directed dimension of "Deep Ecology" (which is in fact the name of the radical environmental philosophy movement discussed here) through courses and workshops. Seed reflects on his activities: "As the implications of evolution and ecology are internalized...there is an identification with life...Alienation subsides..."I am protecting the rainforest" develops to "I am part of the rainforest protecting myself. I am that part of the rainforest recently emerged into thinking".

These are certainly no escapist romanticists, and what they say is not the product of wild imagination. On the contrary: it is based on and fed by a thorough knowledge of natural reality. Moreover, it is becoming recognizable and understandable by a growing number of people, everywhere around us. The wide interest in courses in experience of nature, not only in the United States (whence this movement originated for the most part) but recently in our country as well, is not accidental. Yes, *courses*: we have to undergo training in certain aspects of experience which have been blunted by modern culture if we are to regain full access to them. There is room for development here, in particular of our senses and feelings, not in the last place through environmental and nature *education* explicitly directed at these domains (and not at a mainly cognitively defined relation towards nature only).

The giving of meaning, in this sense, is especially taking place through *direct experience*, and not indirectly, for instance through philosophical or scientific reflection. It is that which does not first pass through the filter of thought. Viewed in this way it is the opposite of a perspective that identifies being human with, or reduces it to, being a "thinking being". Direct experience takes place in one's "soul" or one's feelings, and not so much in one's mind (as an instrument of thought). However, it also takes place in one's body, and this is crucial in ecological spirituality: after all, it is in particular our body which makes us part of our surroundings. Compare the above quotations, often referring to (the permeability of) the skin. The skin is seen here, however, very differently than is usual in philosophical anthropology, not in the first place as a delimitation of or a separation with the environment, but rather as a possible point of interaction, of mutual pervasion.

Corporality can also be viewed as sensuousness, that is *aisthèsis*, in this way directing attention to the *aesthetic*[9] attitude of contemplativity, openness for the other on behalf of itself, that is for its own intrinsic value (these aspects are also discussed by Verkleij and Verhoog elsewhere in this book). This sort of attitude can lead to solidarity which does not draw the other towards oneself or subordinate it in an instrumental way, but lets it be what it is in itself. In other words: it is a *solidarity bridging the distance but maintaining the difference*. This is wonderfully expressed by Lloyd Reinhardt: "To be glad, to rejoice that the other exists, without the desire to consume and possess, these are aspects of an art, the art of letting things be, which is part of the more general and vital human virtue of overcoming the tendency to think of everything in relation to ourselves. It is part of what it is to achieve a degree of what I call, again following Simone Weil, impersonality, a shrinking of the consumptive, aggregative self that we tend most *naturally* to be...The natural order is a natural object for contemplative attention; it can draw someone into some of that attention and into rejoicing in the sheer existence of things,...not because what is there is pretty or nice, merely lovely to look at. It is also perhaps mainly, because it can engender and help sustain a joy in the existence and otherness of things, and in their relations to each other, instead of to oneself; a willingness to let things be what they are, go on in the way they do; even a curiosity to know how things work"[10]. I would not know of a better way to express the contemplative-and-yet-connecting aspect of ecological spirituality.

The importance of science
As has already been said, ecological spirituality is "immanent": solidarity and the giving of meaning refer here (in first instance) to the empirical-factual reality, hence the reality about which science too has something to say. For that reason this spirituality can be promoted and supported by knowledge, scientific knowledge: to really know something about evolution and ecology can help, so to speak, to become overwhelmed by it, and, as a result, one feels

---

9 A theory of ecological aesthetics can be found in my *Participeren aan de natuur*, p. 345-394.
10 L. Reinhardt, On Some Gaps in Moral Space: Reflections on Forests and Feelings, in: D. Mannison et al. (Eds.), *Environmental Philosophy*, Australian National University, Dept. of Philosophy, Canberra, 1980, p. 206-208.

part of that overwhelming reality. I think this is a very important aspect, in particular for modern Western culture. It makes possible a "union of worlds" which once seemed hardly feasible – with the exception perhaps of a 19th century attempt which harvested almost no results: see for example Goethe, discussed also by Verhoog. It appears that we, after passing through the phase of science and rationality, can experience thanks to scientific knowledge something that did seem to have been attainable in earlier times or in other cultures through a religious or metaphysical belief, namely, a spiritual solidarity with nature and with the cosmos as a whole. At the same time, in the last few decades science has also offered opportunities to that end: one no longer only encounters a mechanistic-materialistic-dualistic conception of science in modern physics and biology, but also an organistic-participatory perspective as well.

Nonetheless, science – and certainly not a science of uniform laws determining the behaviour of separate objects – in this way has still not become constitutive for or a touchstone of experience. Experience, as an essential source of all spirituality, always has its own rights, its own validity, its own particularity. However, this does not mean that we have to shut our eyes to the possibilities of contact existing here as well, the helping hand science can sometimes lend (just as the opposite is also possible). For us, for our culture, science can be a supporting condition for ecological experience; it makes it easier for us to view nature in such a way that we feel ourselves to be part of it, and recognize its own value and inherent meaning, to arrive really at a "reenchantment of the world" (Berman). Scientific knowledge, however, is not a necessary precondition for this: nearly all premodern thought managed without it – as do many native cultures still – and there are many people today able to adopt a participatory world view without needing scientific knowledge at all. But for many others this is different, and for our culture as a whole it seems to me that any world view should at least be *consistent* with the results of scientific research, if such a world view is to develop into a socially effective force. We have passed through the phase of rationality and cannot and will not go back on this, so it seems that "as a culture" we have to rely to a certain extent on science in order to feel or experience the solidarity with nature which different or earlier cultures felt and experienced without scientific knowledge, *and* which was socially valid.

I want to stress once more, at this point, that I reject all *scientific reductionism*: the giving of meaning is in itself not dependent on science, nor is it determined by it, and, as I said before, experience has its own rights, its own of abstract laws which can only be grasped through reason. Lastly, it is a science which is not primarily or even exclusively fashioned after the requirements of manipulative interference with nature but which is, at the very least, equally guided by considerations of *contemplativity* and *self-restraint.*

The importance of theology

In ecological spirituality one recognizes a sometimes barely disguised kind of *secular religiosity,* a possibility to give meaning with respect to an all-encompassing whole for those who increasingly are missing this in traditional Christianity, or who perhaps never became aquainted with it (albeit without losing the need for such a meaning-giving solidarity). However, besides this secular dimension, there is also the question of the relationship between ecological spirituality and *non-*secular religiosity, or religious experience. It is of course possible for both of these to exist side by side, and more or less separated from each other. But some people will want to establish links between different domains of the giving of meaning: this is an area in which it would seem particularly difficult to develop far-reaching compartimentalization. Moreover, everyone acknowledging that the world is God's creation, will be confronted by the question of the relationship between this immanent spirituality and the traditional-Christian, transcendent variety.

The main question here is: is it possible to abandon the immanent aspect of ecological spirituality without giving up its ecological dimension? I believe that this is possible provided that two respects of traditional theology are revised, issues I have borrowed as such from the Dutch feminist theologian Catharina Halkes[11]. The first issue is that traditional theology, in her view, places too much emphasis on salvation, liberation from oppression – the tradition of the Covenant – and too little on the blessing acts of God, which are often directly related to nature. Following this, it then becomes possible to understand nature-as-creation not only from the human, that is humanity-related salvation history: it is no longer a derivative but (as regards humanity) an independent entity, with a value in itself, analogous to – in the secular line of thought – an intrinsic value of nature which has not been derived from what is important for humans. This amounts to a theology of creation for the sake of the recognition of the

---

11 C.J.M. Halkes, ...en alles zal worden herschapen; *Gedachten over de heelwording van de schepping in het spanningsveld tussen natuur en cultuur*, Baarn 1990 (1989), p. 94-102 (also in English: Westminster Press/John Knox Press, Louisville, Kentucky).

validity as well. However, science can enhance experience and make it, at least in a number of cases, more specific. It can provide a map of the territory I am traversing, a map which draws my attention to certain things that can be seen there. I will still have to go to that region myself, of course, and I will have to look at it myself: the map as such is not enough, what matters is not the map but the looking, the experience itself. Scientific abstractions are *not* "the real thing": only experienced reality is. Once more: some people do not need a map, at least no scientific map, they do not get lost and they often see a lot of things. Nonetheless, they may still see less than they would do with a map. The need for a map does not always indicate alienation from nature, and, conversely, there is much map-lessly developed "feeling of non-alienation" based for the most part on private imagination only, "subjectivism" without further effects. This however cannot form the foundation of a participatory world view, and it seems to me that it is science in this case which can provide a healthy measure of "objectivism". And yet, not all forms of science can prevent participation being dismissed along with purely subjective fancy.

The nature of this new, "postmodern" science is being discussed at length in many quarters. I will limit myself to some catchwords only. Postmodern science, of course, would have to abstain from analytical reductionism, materialistic mechanicism, and epistemological dualism, at any rate as a dominant perspective. Concerning *nondualism*, I mentioned earlier that emotionality and corporality are important aspects of direct experience, but these can also be seen, in a scientific sense as well, as independent ways of knowing. After all, many aspects of reality conceal themselves from the detached ratio, and why reserve the status of "scientific" (or "scientifically respectable"!) exclusively to all that remains outside these "non-rational" approaches? I mention here for instance Barbara MacClintock's well-known "feeling for the organism" – and did not Augustine already refer to love as the a priori of knowledge ? Next, a truly *ecological organicism*, that is to say recognition of the importance of so-called internal relations on a fundamental, metaphysical level, together with the recognition of self-organization and intentionality at any level. Consequentially we can see evolution not as the result of chance and necessity, but rather as the result of (chance and) purposiveness. Thirdly, it is a science in which the diversity and the interconnectedness of the *phenomenal world* are central: there is a great deal of "phenomenology" in the ecological perspective, as Verhoog rightly argues. This means that the importance of nature is recognized as it appears to the senses, in contrast to the uniformity intrinsic value of nature. However, in my opinion, it will always be an essential aspect of this theology of creation, that creation derives its deepest sense or meaning in its ultimate destination being God: it is for this reason that it has an intrinsic value, or at any rate a value independent of humanity. If this refers, though, to a completely transcendent God, we are not getting any further: just as relating nature to a humanity which is placed outside it undermines nature's intrinsic value, the same thing happens when one relates nature to a God who is placed outside it.

The second issue, then, concerns the rejection of an image of God with an absolutely transcendent character: this only can lead to extricating God from nature and from creation altogether. According to Halkes, however, God is "indwelling" in his creation, and his spirit constitutes the driving force of the world. This view on God's immanence in his creation, that is in nature, is also an important aspect in Verkleij's contribution to this volume. This sort of immanence points in the direction of something like the *sacrality of nature*, however it should be interpreted or even practiced. I don't think this is as unbiblical as many theologians have, until recently, thought it to be, and it is essential if one wants to connect the concept of the intrinsic value of nature to a theology of creation without undermining its intrinsicality. If we then say that it is creation's deepest sense to find its ultimate destination in God, viewed as Himself fully present in this creation or nature, this is something like an ultimate foundation of nature's intrinsically valuable character. Nevertheless, the sacrality of nature remains a difficult issue in every Christian doctrine: while God is "in"(-side) nature, He does not coincide with it, is more than that, and that's why many ecological theologians prefer pan-entheism above pantheism (I understand that Whiteheadian process theology goes beyond this). Compare this, though, with Shiva's description of the fully pantheist *Indian* cosmology. On the other hand: could not, in this ("intercultural") respect, panentheism already seem a tremendous improvement on the absolute transcendence Shiva so rightly criticizes in traditional-modern Christianity?

Nonetheless, it should be clear that even a panentheistic theology is incompatible with the essence of our modern world view: in itself it *is* even its opposite, namely *organicism*, and that in its most far-reaching form. There is a fundamental relationship between an absolute transcendence of God and the mechanistic-materialistic world view, at least as far as history is concerned (I also refer here to Verkleij, who locates this transition to have occurred at the end of the Middle Ages). The theologian John Cobb says that, if one wants to ascribe all (God's) actual acts in the world to an absolutely *transcendent* God, it is inevitable that reality will be deprived of any own purpose, motion, sense. And according to the philosopher Karl Löwith the entire (mechanistic) philosophy of Descartes would not have been possible without this orientation towards a transcendent God. It is also a remarkable fact, that both in modern physics (David Bohm) and in modern biology (Rupert Sheldrake) there has been, from the very beginning, a clear denunciation of this rejection of "working-at-a-distance", this (last) rejection providing the very possibility for an absolutely transcendent God to "work in the world", and – inspired by theology – for centuries seen as a litmus test for being (mechanistically) scientific.

A View on Basic Attitudes towards Nature

Ecological spirituality forms the psychological or experiential component of a fundamental perspective on humanity and nature I call *participatory*. A perspective like this is an example of a *basic attitude*, and the so-called basic attitude approach in environmental philosophy gives the opportunity to enlarge our view in the direction of human acting towards nature, i. e. social practice. This seems to be important if one wants to make a connection between agriculture and spirituality: after all, one needs to know which practical implications certain "spiritual" assumptions can have. An illustration of the practical application of the basic attitude approach in the field of agriculture offers Kockelkoren's philosophical discussion of genetic manipulation of plants, included in this volume[12]. It is remarkable that there exists in The Netherlands a government-backed and -published report like this, exactly in an area viewed by Shiva as an outstanding example of the arrogance of Western application of (agricultural) science. In the following I summarize the basic attitude approach and my own position therein[13], after which I conclude with some remarks on the rootedness in Western history of the partici-

---

12 Other fields where this basic attitude approach has been applied already are for instance water management, environmental utilization space, and nature management.
13 Adapted from: W. Zweers, Radicalism or historical consciousness: on breaks and continuity in the discussion of basic attitudes, in: W. Zweers and J.J. Boersema (Eds.), *Ecology, Technology and Culture; Essays in Environmental Philosophy*, The White Horse Press, Cambridge, 1994, p. 63-72. For a fuller treatment see *Participeren aan de natuur*, Ch. 1.

patory attitude, an attitude which, combined with a spiritual-religious impulse, could be really helpful for an intercultural dialogue.

In basic attitudes towards nature a particular conception about the fundamental structure of reality is expressed: a view or image of the world or of reality as a whole, more specifically an *image of nature*. At the same time there emerges a picture of what it is to be human: who we are, what is important to us, in short a *self image*. The image of nature and the image of self are closely related; they complement one another. I discern six basic attitudes or models:

1. The *despot*, who subjects nature, if necessary by force, and deals with it at will, unhampered by considerations of morality or moderation; in present times this is the technocrat, who has unlimited confidence in technological possibilities, and for whom there are no limits to growth.

2. The *enlightened ruler*, who still reigns over nature, but also recognizes that he is dependent on it; in the interest of realizing human ends he strives towards developing nature's possibilities as much as he can, but he understands that exploitation and oppression are out of the question here.

3. The *steward*, who no longer controls nature on his own authority, but manages it on behalf of the "owner" to whom he is responsible: in the Christian variety that is God, in the secular variety, it is humanity. The tenor is conservative, the emphasis is on conservation of natural resources (i. e. the capital, the interest of which only may be utilized) and the scope is still mainly human-centered.

4. The *partner* works together with nature on the basis of equality, that is in order to realize the "aims" of both parties as well as possible. He strives for integration of fulfilment of social functions and some sort of nature development, both from a dynamic rather than from a static perspective. It is essential to partnership that nature's values and "interests" have now attained equal importance to those of humanity.

5. The *participant*, who views nature as a totality of which he is a part, not only in a biological sense, but especially in the sense that there is an experience of solidarity with nature from which he derives a meaning which is at least contributory to his self-image. He participates in nature, but as an independent being with both identity and culture: he is able to participate in such a way exactly because of his special capacities as a human being (his norms and values).

6. Unity with nature, sometimes referred to as *unio mystica*. The individually experiencing "me" falls away and merges into a nature which in this conception acquires an (immanent) divine character.

The *despot* (or modern technocrat) has been dominant in the development of Western culture since the sixteenth or seventeenth century. This is one of the most important roots of the present environmental crisis, especially in its combination of exclusive orientation towards humanity on the one hand, and reduction of nature to pure factuality and instrumentality on the other hand. Humans see themselves here as the only beings that are more than a resource for others, that is, they are first and foremost valuable for their own right. This can be summarized as *humanity's monopoly on values*, and the consequence is a *fundamentally unique position for humanity*. In this view, humans are placed outside, that is oppose to nature, they are essentially different from it. That is the core of mainstream Western philosophy since Descartes. The *enlightened ruler* and the *steward* can not be considered to be a sufficient answer to the environmental crisis because they are not bringing this *anthropocentrism* to a genuine end. Nevertheless, the latter is attenuated because there is the insight that *nature forms a boundary condition* for realizing human aims and ends: it is in our own interest to take nature into consideration if we want to achieve our aims. There is also the question of *accountability*, maybe to God, in whose name we manage earth, or at any rate to humanity, on behalf of which we manage earth – either spatially, i. e. on a world scale (developing countries), or in time (future generations). The key word here is *sustainability:* sustainable fulfilment of human needs. These two aspects, that of a boundary condition and of accountability, together form the core of reformism, the (theoretical) basis of most recent environmental policy, national and world-wide. However, it still leaves the basis of the despotic-technocratic attitude as I have described it earlier untouched.

Therefore, a radical change in basic attitude is necessary, which is described in the *partner* and *participant* approach. It is "radical" because human monopoly on values and the fundamental opposition between humanity and nature have been broken, and nature is seen as a realm offering meaning and sense to human life. Hence, there are two essential elements of radicalism. Firstly, *breaking the human monopoly on values*, by at least recognizing that there exists something like a *value in nature itself*, that is, that nature is not exhausted by its value for humanity but that it can also have its own "aims", aims which will continue to be present even if humans are not involved in it in any way. This element is emphasized in the partner: here nature makes its own contribution independent of ours, and there is a revaluation, an appreciation of nature even beyond its significance for humanity, though without the implication that humanity and culture should have to undergo a depreciation. Secondly, *breaking the opposition between humanity and nature,* by dispelling the notion that humans are placed fundamentally outside nature. This is emphasized especially by the participant. Participation here is expanded from the biological level of model 2 to the level of meaning and sense. There is an *experience* of solidarity, not merely knowledge of a material connection. This experience is something from which a meaning can be derived that is contributory to what could be meant by "human-ness". These two aspects of radicalism, intrinsic value of nature and solidarity with nature, form two sides of the same coin: solidarity is unthinkable without intrinsic value.

I want to emphasize: rejection of anthropocentrism does not have to lead to (radical) ecocentrism, the latter to be interpreted as man's total subordination to nature. Firstly, with reference to the partner-model: mutually attuning of nature's interests and human interests does not need to mean subordination of the latter. It is not a "zero-sum game" (any more than would be the case in partner relationships between humans). It can mean, however, that we have to restrain ourselves, that we have to set limits to ourselves, but even then our interests and aims will play a full part in the weighing process. However, there is another, perhaps more fundamental consideration, in this case arising from the participation model. The experience of solidarity, participation on the level of meaning and sense, is a specific human ability: it is one of our characteristic capacities which allows us to "belong to nature" in this way. Other natural beings know of participation on a biological level only: this level is also applicable to us, but we are capable of more. This leads me to a sort of paradox: thanks to that which differentiates us from other natural beings, it is possible for us to belong to nature in a more encompassing way than the merely biological, at least if we choose to do so. That means at the very least a subordination or neglect of what is human. On the contrary, this is full participation as a human being, with the identity of someone who is in possession of human norms and values (including norms like social justice, political equality and economic fairness on a world scale). One could also say, "Noblesse oblige".

Participation as a human being also means that one strives towards one's own aims, with the help of science, technology and rationality (albeit these in a transformed way). This perspective of participation is in no way hostile towards these human capacities or towards the enlightened self interest which they support or towards the interfering with nature necessary for man to survive. However, there is a very important limiting factor: these specifically human aims must not be a last resort, or obtain an absolute character, but should always be imbedded in the encompassing notion of participation, which places them in a limiting framework.

Such pursuit of one's own ends, not in an absolute way but from a participatory position, could be called pursuing from within, in contrast to controlling from without. Other natural beings also pursue their aims from within, by definition, so to speak, because they belong to nature. However, in the case of humans, we can say that if we place ourselves outside nature with respect to meaning and sense, following the fundamental misconception of a great deal of modern Western philosophy, the pursuit of our ends will attain an absolute character: it will become a pursuit through domination from outside, which will lead to the destruction of nature (and, in the end, of man also). Therefore, the alternative does not have to be at all incompatible with our enlightened self interest, the latter is only restricted. One can see, then, that the recognition of nature's intrinsic value, together with the realization that we belong to nature, is a way of restricting the pursuit of our own aims. It is a concept that lays a sort of minimal condition for what may and can be done to nature, just as is the case in relationships between humans.

Ecological radicalism and Western history

Radicalism as interpreted above does not have to mean a wholesale rejection of Western cultural history. While duly acknowledging all the differences, it can quite well be viewed as a return to certain elements of "premodern" thinking, where the world is conceived of as an organized and meaningful entity in itself, which is subjected to "spiritual" principles, an entity within which humans occupy a specific place and which forms the basis for their understanding of themselves. Because nature and spirit had not yet taken up such sharply opposed positions, it was possible for man, also a spiritual being, to take part in that world on more than just a material, biological level. Karl Löwith[14], calls this view "cosmotheological": man understands himself within the framework of an immanently, divinely ordered world, a cosmos, an order existing by and on behalf of itself, neither created by a transcendent God outside it nor imposed in a dominating manner by humanity in conflict with it. Human destiny is therefore to achieve a harmonious concordance with this order, especially by way of actions whose fulfilment is found within themselves: contemplative,

---

14 K. Löwith, Gott, *Mensch und Welt in der Metaphysik von Descartes bis zu Nietschze,* Göttingen 1967, p. 9-24.

reflective, even "aesthetic", and not interfering, transforming, converting to man's sole will. Finally, that this is a possibility at all, may be seen as a privilege of humanity, which may indeed be placed within this order, but which nevertheless finds itself in a privileged position within this whole.

This is easily interpreted as a description of the participation model proposed above, and this is what I have in mind when I say that ecological radicalism has historical roots. What in my opinion truly has no tradition, is rather the modern, mathematical-mechanistic-technocratic world view: this is almost literally "without example", not only from a historical but perhaps also from a geographical-cultural point of view. The premodern concept of nature has been totally lost in our times: the spiritual is concentrated in humanity, and only the material has been left for nature, and that is the core of the present day concept of nature, which makes it impossible for us to relate to nature in any other way than from the outside. According to Löwith, this modern world view has been fostered and made possible by Christianity since Augustine, particularly in its characteristic moving towards the self-experience by humanity of an exclusively transcendent God, and the renouncing of the world, which in this way becomes something unimportant or accidental: "ein Uebriges", as Löwith says. Humanity thus no longer understands itself from the perspective of the world as described above, but rather from that of God, and the world disappears behind any horizon of sense or meaning. Without this latter development, the idea of placing humanity outside the world, which is so typical of modern thinking, could not have originated. When, along with the process of secularization, God himself finally disappears behind the horizon too, human self-experience is left as the only basis for our self-understanding and world view. From now on humanity is able to understand itself and the world from its own standpoint only.

It seems to me that ecological radicalism is now once more trying to include the world in the "triangle of meaning". However, this does not have to conflict with a renewed (immanent) understanding of God in any way (as is exemplified in the various forms of ecological theology). Neither need this occur at the expense of humanity. Quite the contrary, it is not a matter of *choosing between* the three realms of meaning "Gott, Mensch und Welt" (Löwith): in the end we need them *all* for a truly human existence. To refer once more to the idea of basic attitudes: we do not only need a radical change of our image of nature and our image of man – the two constituents of a basic attitude in its first, secular instance – but perhaps of our image of God as well

– as a possible third constituent of a basic attitude: in its last instance, so one could say rightly.

It is here that perhaps a common and workable basis could be found for an intercultural dialogue really deserving its name. If we could succeed, in our own Western way, in restoring something of what we seem to have eradicated completely at first in ourselves and subsequently in many parts of the non-Western world as well, i. e. fulfilment of the entire triangle of meaning consisting of God, man and nature, only then we would be able (and entitled) to associate on equal terms with other cultures with regard to an essential aspect of human-ness. After all, as I said before, exactly in that respect we rather still belong ourselves to the developing countries indeed.

APPENDIX 1

Ethical Aspects of Plant Biotechnology

Report for the Dutch Government Commission on Ethical Aspects of Biotechnology in Plants

Petran Kockelkoren

I Introduction

Biotechnology evokes mixed feelings with the general public. On the one hand, great expectations have been raised: biotechnology is reputedly capable of bringing about a revolutionary improvement in the world food supply and in the production of medicines. On the other hand, the new opportunities raise fears. If it becomes possible to tamper with the genetic code, which many consider the blueprint for life, what kind of a world are we entering? Will everything now be subject to the caprice of human desires? It is clear that this new technique raises fundamental questions.

Although generally conscious of such fears, the proponents of biotechnology believe that they can be scaled down to a realistic and acceptable scepticism. Though relatively new, the techniques are not radically different from already accepted and applied techniques. As a consequence, the risks are predictable, at least to a certain extent, and definitely not as frightening as the ominous forecasts some opponents suggest. Even if the high hopes are realized only in part, biotechnology could bring relief. With a growing world population, we simply cannot afford to ignore this promise to ease the world food problem. Yet there are people who feel these arguments, accurate though they may be, lead them to a critical zone of their sense of propriety. The pace of technological developments threatens to outstrip the moral debate.

Indeed biotechnology, among other issues, brings to the surface a clash between the scientific and technical world view on the one hand and age-old views on the place of man in nature on the other. Historically, the order of species in nature has been considered sacrosanct. It was the aim of science and technology to lay bare the laws of nature in order to take advantage of them, but not to alter them at will. This now seems to be changing. In nature, horizontal gene transfer, i.e. gene transfer in the series plants-animals-humans, hardly occurs spontaneously, but is made possible by biotechnology. The question is, are we ready to cross this boundary? Such questions touch upon the roots of many people's world view. Even if the risks involved are of a level that has long been accepted in other fields, the question remains whether we should consent to this particular development. While the proponents of this technology are pleading for research to uncover the real risks, so that we may know what to say Yes or No to, a broad group in society raises the preliminary question of whether such research is desirable in the first place. Therefore under the pressure of new technological developments, we cannot therefore escape the debate on the foundations of our world view. Meanwhile, scientific and technological research continues. This is inevitable. In our culture the gaining of scientific insight is held in high esteem. It would be absurd to prohibit the human curiosity for the workings of nature. After all, biotechnology does not make any empty promises; in all probability, it can really make a contribution towards alleviating the distress of people and animals. What is needed is to initiate a debate that guides the technological developments. The aim of this should not be to make a moral judgment, either in favour of or against biotechnology, for that would mean that the messenger of the clash of world views would himself have to bear the burden. Instead, a moral debate should keep pace with developments in the research field and consider the different issues involved, consulting with researchers, ethicists, politicians and representatives of societal organizations.

In the Netherlands, this debate is well under way. The question of the moral boundaries in biotechnology in animals led to a public discussion that took place from 14 to 16 May 1993 in The Hague. Commissioned by the Ministry of Agriculture, Nature Management and Fisheries, a report was produced by the Schroten Committee on Ethics and Biotechnology in Animals which produced a test criterion. Reduced to a formula, that criterion is "Only subject to certain conditions". Following on from that public and political discussion, the need was felt to pay attention also to the moral aspects of biotechnology applications in plants.

It is natural to refer to the moral framework constructed for animal biotechnology when looking to answer moral questions on biotechnology in plants. However, this approach is fraught with problems. Applying human moral principles to animals may have been difficult, but is made defensible by addressing "welfare" in both humans and animals. With respect to plants, however, "welfare" is a doubtful basis of approach. For this reason, some argue that applying ethical principles to plants is nonsense. Nonetheless, the integrity of species is at stake and thus the degradation of the natural order – however this is viewed – no less in plants than in animals and human beings. If we want to tackle these questions, we will first have to formulate the terms in which a normative debate can be held, as ethics with respect to plants cannot simply be a derivative of that for humans and animals.

The committee set up to supervise the preliminary investigation into ethical aspects of plant biotechnology agreed, after careful consideration, not to aim for the formulation of test criteria. The task description drawn up by the Ministry of Agriculture, Nature Management and Fisheries did not require that. The aim was rather to set out the perspectives for a moral review. As the participants in the public and political debate look at the matter from different points of view, it is useful to make an inventory of the different languages they speak. By mapping the various viewpoints and the concepts used to express them, the current confusion of tongues may be resolved. Only then can we hope that a continued debate may bring about a consensus, also with regard to test criteria.

The supervisory committee for the investigation in question was of mixed membership. On it served people from different representative camps: researchers from companies, universities and government institutes, policy-making civil servants and representatives of the environmental movement. This variety enabled the investigator to make an inventory of possible viewpoints on the basis of bilateral conversations with committee members. The next step was to infer "fundamental attitudes" from the various viewpoints and their problem definitions. Fundamental attitudes were more appropriate as an intermediary concept than "frameworks of interpretation" because positions on biotechnology in humans, animals and plants do not just revolve around concepts but also involve a moral orientation.

The following fundamental attitudes towards nature are distinguished: domination, stewardship, partnership and participation. In this report, the inventory of fundamental attitudes is presented with the accompanying views on nature and the moral position on a number of topical issues relevant to plant biotechnology, such as: herbicide resistance, resistance against biotic factors (disease), resistance against abiotic factors (cold, drought, salt tolerance), aesthetic change (shape, colour, smell, taste), introduction of alien components in species, economic protection through patents, and through plant breeder's rights.

This report consists of the following parts: first, common pros and cons of biotechnology are listed (II), followed by arguments underpinning the need of a differentiated ethical language (III). Then the historical technological developments in agriculture are reviewed, from the perspective of the gradual change in attitude to nature, up to current biotechnology as a provisional end point (IV). Next the fundamental attitudes are introduced to enable the required differentiated ethical review (V). With these as points of reference, a number of issues in plant biotechnology can be judged from different ethical points of view (VI). Some conclusions and recommendations conclude the report (VII).

II Intrinsic versus Extrinsic Arguments

Some say that biotechnology enables us to intervene in nature in a manner that is unprecedented. The present state of biotechnology is then represented as the provisional outcome of a spontaneous evolutionary process. The opponents of biotechnology denounce this intervention as the dangerous pride of technology. They fear an uncontrollable advance in the artificial generation of new species with hitherto unknown combinations of properties. The introduction of new crop plants might lead to a reduction in spontaneous biodiversity when the wild varieties are squeezed out by crop plants.

However, the proponents of biotechnology do not agree with the implicit distinction between spontaneous genesis in nature and artificial generation through technology. Plant improvement has been undertaken by humans since prehistoric times, resulting in the present-day crop species. All biotechnology does is continue this age-old improvement with the help of more precise technology. There is nothing new in that.

Obviously, these preliminary verbal stabs from both camps are only rough thrusts. The brunt of the duel is fought out with shows of expertise and counter-expertise. This outline of arguments already shows that the camps adhere to different views of nature. On one side, nature is seen as to have been there before culture and now to be threatened by it, especially when the cultural influence is strengthened by technology. On the other side, it is thought that nature has always manifested itself through culture, and even technology. We will shed more light on the views of nature with the introduction of the fundamental attitudes. It may be noted here that the debate is often deadlocked by such a confusion of concepts. In order to get rid of the deceptive controversies in the principle moral debate, we will start by setting out the promised blessings of biotechnology together with the feared dangers.

What are the benefits that are attributed to plant biotechnology? Without entering into details, the following breakthroughs are being proposed:
– New forms of disease and pest resistance in plants.
– A reduction of the burden on the environment by the development of herbicide-resistant crops that require a reduced pesticide input, more biodegradable into the bargain.
– The development of ecologically harmless crop supporting organisms such as genetically engineered insects or bacteria with favourable characteristics for plants, such as frost resistance and drought resistance.
– Greater yields, i.e. an increased food supply for the rapidly growing world population, providing such an intensification of agriculture does not cause a heavy burden on the environment through soil degradation and pesticides.
– Improved processability and storage life of products, e.g. in interruption of the ripening process in tomatoes.
– New colours, smells, and tastes to benefit the satisfaction of our aesthetic and gastronomical needs.
– Development of new medicines or, for example, the generation of organic medicines in bacterial cultures instead of their troublesome and limited (and thus expensive) production from living or dead humans and animals.
It is obvious that the benefits listed are of completely different natures. Environmental arguments are juxtaposed with economic benefits and culinary delights are placed side by side with medicinal products. Some benefits seem to stand out among the list for their advantages for man and environment and their moral justifiability.

What are the fears that rise in connection with plant biotechnology? A similarly concise overview will suffice:
– Disturbance of the balance of existing ecosystems through introduction of new species or of artificial varieties of species (genetically coded for disease and pest resistance) that could have evolutionary advantages in relation to their so-called "wild" congeners.
– An infringement of the natural order (the creation or the product of evolution) of which the consequences are without precedent and not to be foreseen.
This applies in particular to gene transfer between non-related species.

– An increase rather than a decrease of the burden on the environment, caused by:

    a introduction of alien gene combinations that require an adjusted environment or that bring about such an environment through unequal competition;

    b genetic erosion as a consequence of the large-scale monocultures being required to make the investment in the technological approach economically profitable;

    c excessive rather than reduced use of pesticides because the then resistant plants are unaffected.

– Intensification of the economic competition between world powers rather than a trend break, because of:

    a the increasing grip of multinationals (seed companies, pesticide producers and insurance companies) on the food supply;

    b growing dependence of Third World farmers on seed improvers in the industrialized world as their home-produced seed is no longer competitive; this leads to a more and more uniform food supply;

    c replacement of agricultural raw materials by artificial varieties (e.g. aspartame as sugar cane replacement) causing Third World farmers to lose business;

    d the wealthy industrialized world's control of the world gene pool (medicinal plants from the Third World are being biotechnologically improved and then patented, leaving the original discoverers in the country of origin empty-handed).

– Is the world food problem the result of food scarcity or is the scarcity the result of the economic state of affairs and concomitant maldistribution? In the latter case the introduction of capital intensive cultivation methods means deterioration rather than improvement. What is being presented as a solution will only serve to aggravate the evil.

The drawbacks listed are also of different kinds: they vary from ecological to economic arguments, while implicit notions of "naturalness" feature as well (the more spontaneous biodiversity the better).

To bring order in the diversity of arguments a recent philosophical and ethical study carried out for the UK chemical and seed company ICI has employed the distinction of arguments of an "intrinsic" and an "extrinsic" nature.[1] We will use this distinction too, albeit with a slightly different definition to extend its usefulness.

The arguments based on intrinsic nature have to do with respect for "naturalness" (which can be articulated further in different ways). Applied to ethical aspects of plant biotechnology, this could be understood as respect for the integrity of the plant species in question. The supposed integrity will then be associated with the completeness of the life cycle. This cycle may be guided, or even accelerated or enriched, but, as in the interruption of the ripening process, not interrupted by technical means. On the basis of this criterion, many conventional breeding techniques are also targeted. Biotechnology is developing an established practice to excess, calling for a review of agriculture and horticulture in general (even with retroactive effect).

The arguments based on extrinsic nature refer to the potential ecological and social consequences of plant biotechnology. One such consequence is the risk of diffusion of genetically modified crops into the environment, which could result in evolutionary advantages for artificial varieties of a species. Other consequences are: the risk of transfer of resistance through spontaneous cross-pollination to wild species, economic consequences for the Third World, and patent problems.

The ICI study implies that concern for intrinsic aspects is primarily a philosophical and religious matter, which we can safely leave to the Churches, while the extrinsic consequences are to be dealt with by politicians, who may call on scientists and technologists for information. Presented in this way, the required ethical reconsideration of our moral starting-points is automatically phrased in terms of risk analyses. And in reality that is happening across the board. The OECD uses the "familiarity principle"; risks incurred by biotechnology are acceptable if, according to current scientific standards, they do not exceed the risks of conventional techniques. Analogous to the familiarity principle is the criterion of "substantial equivalence" used with reference to the composition of products. Genetically modified products are acceptable as long as they do not exceed the accepted threshold value for toxic substances in food and luxury products (tomatoes, coffee, tobacco, etc.).

Despite the fact that there will always be an unpredictable aspect, because the consequences in the evolutionary term can never be foreseen, many accept risk assessment rather than ethics as a pragmatic basis for provisional regulation. And it goes a long way. Genetic modification will mostly be applied to crops that have been used for centuries, the potential risks being largely familiar. Besides, the risks seem to closely resemble the well-known risks of the introduction of exotics. The chance of a non-pathogenic crop becoming pathogenic with the modification of only a few genes is largely imaginary. Through measures to restrict the risks, such as using closed green-houses and cutting off seed buds, unforeseen side-effects may surface in time so that they become controllable. A similar reasoning is applied to the social and economic risks – through legislation and regulation as well as adequate enabling policies these seem to be equally controllable.

These attempts to scale down the problem to manageable proportions, if this can be done at all, are not very helpful in entering upon a moral review. The starting point of such a review should be the very consideration of what is at stake in recognizing intrinsic qualities. Respect for intrinsic qualities may prevent or reduce the occurrence of extrinsic consequences. In any case, this discussion is as vital for political decision-making as the discussion on risk control, and the former even deserves to take place prior to the latter. We must first decide whether we want something before we consider to what extent we want it. The debate has to differentiate between various applications and the various reasons for and against. In order to clarify what we can and what we cannot expect of ethics, we will now start by considering our ethical starting-points, with specific reference to ethical aspects of plant biotechnology.

III The Need for a Set of Pluralistic Ethics

Ethics makes up the body of moral principles, or values, that we choose to live by. Which values do we place first? Few values are so sacrosanct that they never have to make way for other values. The current morality is the outcome of a previous weighing of values which introduced a certain scale of priorities. Morality not only supplies a provisional scale of values, but also states which means are permitted for realizing these values. As long as we act within the bounds of this morality there is bound to be a consensus on the propriety of our action. A review of the moral principles will only be undertaken when serious doubts are raised as to the prevailing value scale.

Recent technological developments are putting current morality to the test. They call for a review of the scale of values that form the pillars of our society. Our concept of nature is about to change. Both nature's intrinsic value (if any) and human dignity in relation to nature are under discussion. Recent developments, in gene technology in particular, demand a re-evaluation of our basic principles. The trust in the compass of morality has to make way for ethical reflection upon the sustainability of this morality.

The intrinsic value of nature is almost completely overlooked in the prevailing morality. This morality originated in the spirit of the anthropocentric Age of Enlightenment. In this perspective the moral community consists solely of accountable individuals. As far as morals are concerned, only humans are relevant. When these moral principles were first formulated, even the definition of who was human was narrow. The great philosopher Kant acknowledged human rights, but when he applied this position to civil rights only the propertied class really counted – the poor, slaves, women and children being excluded. Since that time, the abolition of slavery, the introduction of women's suffrage and the prohibition of child labour have effected a gradual shift towards inclusion of a wider circle in the moral community. The next shift of boundaries is to be in the direction of animal rights, subsequently plants.[2]

However, in including plants in the moral community, the ethical standard rooted in the Enlightenment loses its validity. In the tradition of the Age of Reason, the moral community was circumscribed by the presence of a mutual responsibility between autonomous individuals. This clause does not apply to animals and plants. Humans may have some responsibility towards animals and plants, but there is no question of reciprocal animal or plant responsibility towards humans or among animals and/or plants. They thus do not belong to the domain of modern morality.

However, with a little adjustment morality can be stretched, extending its domain while maintaining its underlying principles. This is possible because there is some measure of correspondence between the human and animal physical condition and their capacity for suffering. Children and the mentally retarded also belong to the moral community, although they cannot reciprocate our responsibility for them. We do, however, feel that we have a moral responsibility to care for them. By analogy, this care is then extended to animals. Extending this analogy to plants would be to stretch it beyond credibility. Animal welfare can reasonably be discussed, but plant welfare is contestable.

A set of ethics aiming to embrace the integrity of plant life as a principle will have to come up with new basic principles and introducing new categories. Debate on this point requires willingness to learn a new ethical language – a language which does not take human welfare *a priori as* the point of departure, with other forms of life featuring at lower levels. An investigation into the ethical aspects of plant biotechnology will therefore have to start with a search for new terms.

Not everybody would subscribe to that analysis. A prominent argument advanced by the supporters of biotechnology is that biotechnology is much different from already accepted and widely applied breeding techniques, regulation of which apparently was not impossible within the bounds of current morality. This position stresses the above-mentioned concepts of the "familiarity principle" and the standard of "substantial equivalence". As this is a perilous undertaking to be avoided where possible, it is unnecessary and even undesirable to redefine our ethical base. As long as there is a consensus, nothing should be done to upset its foundations. Biotechnology contributes towards mitigating the world food problem. The extrinsic consequences – the risks and even the mechanisms of devolution towards the Third World – are in principle politically controllable under current morality. Under these circumstances there is, in the opinion of the supporters of biotechnology, insufficient reason to start modifying the ethical principles themselves.

This line of reasoning can however be reversed. The view that biotechnology does not essentially differ from other modern techniques can lead to the conclusion that those techniques can equally not be allowed to escape an ethical review of our relationship to nature. It is possible that in the course of our cultural development we have overlooked switches that may still have to be turned. In this perspective, biotechnology is the extreme consequence of an approach to nature which is now raising doubts as to its ethical tenability.

The foregoing discussion should not be understood as a direct threat to biotechnology or even existing agricultural technologies. A review of ethical principles is about which values we want to recognize and in which order. Even if we were from now on to recognize intrinsic values in nature, this would not mean that they might never be violated. At most that there would have to be good reasons for doing so. What we would need are criteria to differentiate between acceptable and unacceptable technologies. With regard to plants this means in the first place that respect for their intrinsic value will have to be formulated and recognized, and that the ethical implications will have to be worked out.

The current public and political debate elicited by present-day biotechnology takes place between representatives of different ethical denominations, each speaking a different ethical language and assigning different priorities in the weighing of values. A study that sets out to map the various options and their relative merits will have to cover much cultural and historical ground. What are the contours of the current morality and what will change when, besides taking man as the exclusive starting-point, we start to consider the intrinsic value of other forms of life as an additional starting-point? Such theorizing can bring about a shift in the ethical viewpoint from "anthropocentric" to "ecocentric". Much would be gained if it became clear that to assign a more dignified status to plants is not necessarily to ascribe human properties to plants; rather it is to curtail the authority of human action with respect to other forms of life on the grounds of their intrinsic value.

The transformation from the present anthropocentric attitude to a more ecocentric one, or even small steps in this direction, can only happen if this is a tendency in society at large. This may reside in the more or less collective fundamental attitudes that guide us in our ethical choices. Some groups in society tend to be anthropocentric in their fundamental attitude and others ecocentric, with all kinds of intermediate varieties. Before presenting a survey of these fundamental attitudes, it may be important to know what is at stake, and what choices society is being required to make concerning the future development of agriculture. A concise historical overview of agricultural developments may serve to clarify what has to be decided on the basis of various fundamental attitudes, and what values are involved.

IV Continuity or Break in the Development of Agricultural Techniques?

Proponents of biotechnology, referring to the relationship between biotechnology and modern breeding techniques having already found public acceptance, emphasize the continuity with traditional agriculture. This seems an apologetic strategy, because there is at least equal reason to highlight the discontinuity. After all, the traditional methods of cultivation and breeding are generally set in sharp contrast with modern agriculture. To be able to judge the extent of continuity or discontinuity with tradition, and to be able to decide whether, in case of continuity, we wish to carry on as we are, we need a necessarily brief synopsis of cultural history.

Traditional and modern society are contrasted in the form of typically ideal descriptions. Traditional society is based on solidarity: although shortages can occur, these are shared equally within an extensive and finely meshed system of family relationships. Nature – if not in totality, nevertheless in its constituent parts such as plants and animals – is seen as a co-subject. Plants and animals belong to the family, as it where. Traditional farming takes place within the world of perception: improvement envisages an optimized balance between crops and the environment given. To that end, the seasonal cycle is followed faithfully. Improvement is achieved by selecting seed from strong plants.

This traditional model of the relation between culture and nature was replaced by the modern (economic) model. The switch from a traditional to a modern society occurs when solidarity makes way for competition. Surplus production is sold and no longer used to make up shortages elsewhere within one's own broad circle. The fact that not everybody continues to share in well-being or want is not however attributed to social interrelationships, but nature is blamed as the parsimonious supplier of food. Nature does not offer enough for everybody. "Shortage" is the key concept in modern society, where personal relationships become externalized, everybody fends for themselves, and everybody tries to keep shortage at bay. The fact that this attitude does not degenerate into universal warfare is due to a collective battle against the parsimony of nature.

The introduction of economic relationships had a major impact on the relationship between culture and nature. What used to be common land was abolished and passed into private ownership. Family estates became marketable cadastral plots. This logically resulted in land reform in support of more efficient farm management. The landscape became more uniform, a process which did not remain limited to town and country planning but became reflected in other cultural spheres as well. Local dialects and the popular wisdom they contained concerning the local attachment with the environment were lost in the formation of a general vernacular.

This overall levelling process also affected agriculture. Specialization took place in order to be able to meet market demand. Processing into branded products requires standardization of raw materials. For this purpose, both the environment (by the use of soil conditioners and artificial fertilizers) and the organisms are manipulated. Agriculture underwent major changes with the increasing advent of science. The discoveries made by Darwin and Mendel led to a tremendous increase in the speed of conventional breeding techniques. The large-scale creation of new species by means of selective cross-breeding and selection was undertaken in a scientific way. Crop improvement has taken place since neolithic times: our cereal crops, for example, are the product of many centuries' application of traditional methods. In such cases, we refer to "native species". While the native species were the products of local crop improvement and therefore had a limited area of distribution because they were adapted to specific environments, in the process of modernization the "breeders' varieties" appeared on the scene. The breeders' varieties have been rendered largely independent of local environments, in other words soil type, humidity, climate and the seasonal cycle of the plant. Besides hybridization, since the beginning of the twentieth century the heterosis effect has also been exploited, which means the increased hybrid vigour which occurs in a cross between two genetically different lines. This approach is already fairly remote from the traditional cultivation method.

If we now wish to define the position of biotechnology in the development as outlined, it appears that although continuity must be present within an extended development of modernization, over a longer time-scale the effects of a former discontinuity are nevertheless rapidly being intensified. This is illustrated by the fact that the modern "breeders' varieties" have recently begun to be replaced by "world varieties". Breeding companies stand to gain if their varieties can be given maximum independence of geographical differences in environment, as this is the only way that they can enlarge the market for their products. Two strategies are available: either they attempt to render genotypal expression environment-independent by seeking generalists; this is the route from native species to breeders' species (from the regional to the European scale). Or they can attempt to produce a uniform cultivation environment, crop breeding focusing on adapting the plant to a single standard environment. In this case, breeding concentrates on the development of specialists. This is already being done to some extent by means of selective fertilizer and spray regimes, and on a very large scale in mineral substrate cultivation. Of course, there is more potential scope for this in horticulture than in agriculture. Such a disengagement from geographical differences completes the transition from breeders' varieties to world varieties. The variety now is exported together with its ideal environment. Breeding relates both to crop and the environment.

In the second strategy, however, the focus of crop improvement differs in effect from the first strategy, namely on specialists other than generalists, and it is particularly at that point where biotechnology contributes. For example, genetic modification influencing the freezing point or introducing salt tolerance in crops, combined with a standardized environment, enables these particular varieties to attain an unprecedented distribution. In this way, biotechnology radicalizes the modern trend towards increasing disengagement of crops from geographical differences in environment.

This can be further clarified by making a brief introduction to the biological principles involved. Plants are distinguished from animal and human organisms by their "totipotence", that is to say, complete plants can be generated not only from reproductive organs but, in principle, from all cells. In the traditional approach, this makes it possible to take cuttings, and in the modern scientific approach it enables the practice of cloning. A fairly novel technique in biotechnology is the production of somatic embryos: based on a plant cell, a tissue culture is initiated which – provided with added nutrients and an encapsulation – can function as an artificial seed. From such seeds, descendants are obtained which are genetically identical to the plant from which the initial cell was isolated. This asexual propagation technique guarantees series of identical plants.

In addition, in order to be sure of obtaining equal expression of the genetic starting material in all these identical descendants, the environment is preferably maintained in an artificially invariant state by cultivation on mineral substrate or in hydrocultures. Whereas plants, of their own nature, form an expression of the constantly changing relationship between genes and local environment, in the new cultivation technique the environment factor is virtually totally standardized. Application of that technique is to a large extent environmentally neutral. Large-scale application of genetically modified crops has aroused the fear that it will cause the destruction of a large diversity of local varieties, especially in the Third World; this is known as "genetic erosion".

In view of the growing "abstraction" from the environment, critics claim that the biotechnological approach to nature is "exclusive and reducing DNA-thinking".[3] A plant's link with its environment is broken, and the environment itself may be replaced by a technologically controlled virtual reality for the plant involved. In the extreme case, biotechnologically produced food supply could be totally based on glasshouse production – a prospect that is even welcomed by a number of critics of culture in the nature conservancy sector. They propose that the world food supply should be concentrated in glasshouse cultures, so that the area of land available for agriculture can be reduced in favour of a newly developing nature. Of course, this representation is based on an overstatement. Most proponents of biotechnology envisage their products being integrated as part of the Broodtekst field cropping programme. Although they focus much attention on the potential risks arising from possible undesirable distribution, nevertheless, the macro-consequences in the social sphere, in particular for the Third World, represent an obstacle. In the meantime, however, the first cautious signs of a sea-change are emerging. The Brundtland report, published under the auspices of the United Nations, has received wide acclaim. The pursuit of "sustainable development" is also a high priority in agriculture policy. Although the term "sustainable development" is based on two virtually incompatible concepts, namely that of economic development and that of sustainable nature management, it provides us with a yardstick by which we can compare different classes of technology with one another. Although sustainable development in the absolute sense is scarcely if at all attainable, nevertheless it provides some indication as to "more or less in the right direction". Measured against this yardstick, biotechnological applications leading to global monocultures of crops are immediately ruled out. In that respect, the decision has already been taken internationally to break with the modern trend. However, biotechnology is also capable of making a contribution towards diversification of crops in matching them to specific environments. That is also a process demonstrably taking place. Worldwide research projects already contrast with large numbers of small-scale applications specifically tailored to farming in developing countries. The line of development from native varieties via breeders' varieties to world varieties is therefore not inevitable; on the contrary, changes of direction are already becoming apparent.

In these reflections, it will have become clear what choices have to be made and what values are at stake. The ethical assessment of developments in biotechnology will have to be made with reference to whether they are compatible with the image of sustainable development. The notion of respect for the integrity of plant life can draw due attention to the environmental component in making that assessment. With reference to the ecological importance of local varieties, the search must be made for greater diversity, not in universal relationships but in specific relationships between variety and environment. Also in the interests of Third World farmers, small-scale applications at the local level are preferable to large-scale projects. Just how these limitations and opportunities will be appreciated by groups representing different fundamental attitudes, each with their own specific view of nature, remains to be seen.

V Fundamental Attitudes with Regard to Nature

By means of fundamental attitude, we position ourselves emotionally in the world, somewhere in a precarious equilibrium between remoteness and involvement. Fundamental attitudes are basic value orientations which guide us in our interpretations of the world. They are therefore the source of our mental images or thoughts, and form dispositions to action. Starting from concepts of nature, we can check back to the underlying fundamental attitudes. The relevant concepts must be representative. Initially, they are defined according to typical ideals, as was done above in contrasting traditional and modern society. The term "ideal type" originates from Max Weber, who considers that social reality is replete with meanings. If we want to understand this reality, we must make a selective cross-section by drawing up a suitable ideal type.

The fundamental attitudes sought are linked in a special way to the typically ideal concepts of nature presented here. Depending on the fundamental attitude only certain cross-sections of meaning will be accessible to us. In one fundamental attitude (namely domination) it will be, above all, meanings of cultural origin that emerge, while in the extreme opposite case (namely participation) it will be mainly nature meanings.

The art of interpreting meanings is called "hermeneutics". Coupled to that, fundamental attitudes could be regarded as hermeneutic keys. The various fundamental attitudes open different access roads to nature (understood as a "semantic context") and accordingly different concepts of nature correspond with them.[4] As there is a direct correlation between fundamental attitudes and images of nature, they can both be plotted on an axis, the two extremes being "anthropocentrism" at one end and "ecocentrism" at the other. The first variant is called "domination", the opposing variant "participation". In the domination attitude, nature is assigned a functional value which has its origin in culture. In the participation attitude, the intrinsic value of nature is recognized and culture is assumed to comply. Between the two extremes, a position on the axis is marked to represent the partnership attitude: there an attempt is made to make the functional assignment of value and the recognition of intrinsic value mutually compatible. In view of its extensive and historically influential nature, there is a special variant of fundamental attitude that calls for special mention: stewardship. The steward is situated between the dominator and the partner. This accountability should be expressed in all spheres of life for which accountability is due. Generally for religious reasons (accountability towards the Creator) but also from comparable secular motives (accountability towards future generations), the steward accepts the duty to care for nature. The steward is therefore anthropocentric, but takes care of nature insofar as any form of intrinsic value is recognizable in it.

Accordingly, four fundamental attitudes are distinguished in a range running from anthropocentrism to ecocentrism. The debate on fundamental attitudes was introduced into environmental philosophy in the Netherlands by Zweers.[5] He distinguishes six fundamental attitudes in the same range. Lest the extremes become caricatured, he names two additional "outposts": the "despot" on the side of the dominator, and the "unio mystica" on the side of participation. This releases the domination attitude from the odium of tyranny over nature; the dominator is introduced as an enlightened ruler. In the same movement, the participant is freed from mythical or natural religious characteristics. We confine ourselves to four fundamental attitudes, but preserve the sympathetic view of dominator and participant.

One fundamental attitude is no less ethically justified than another. All four are ethical points of departure, only they proceed under different signs. Below, an attempt is made to define the value of specific biotechnological applications as seen from the various fundamental attitudes. This method is intended to clarify the ethical debate between the representatives of the various fundamental attitudes, not to make a judgment of Solomon on who is ultimately in the right. Assessing the merits of the fundamental attitudes is left to public debate and – following that – to politics. Incidentally, the attempt made here to assign policy relevance to thinking in terms of fundamental attitudes should not be allowed to arouse the impression that the variety of fundamental attitudes in themselves should be defined in terms of a different appropriation of resources for each attitude. Rather, an outline of the content of fundamental attitudes precedes the attempt to identify their policy relevance. A brief definition of the four various fundamental attitudes, focused on the problems of cultural history with which biotechnology confronts us, as observed above, therefore serves as a first step towards an ethical assessment on a number of separate problem areas of biotechnology in the vegetable kingdom.

A. The Dominator
– The dominator believes that nature is completely at his disposal in support

of the continued existence of the human race. Nature therefore is merely a source of raw materials, functionally related to human goals. The dominator's attitude is dynamic, for in his appropriation and improvement of nature he is constantly pushing back frontiers. The dominator seeks maximum utility and profit; at the same time he observes democratically the boundary conditions of the existing legal and economic system. By its unpredictable aspects (earthquakes, floods, plagues) the dominator views nature as something to be conquered and controlled. Nature is best enjoyed in domesticated form. Left to itself, living nature follows a course of trial and error by the process of natural selection. In this way, successful genotypes become dominant. Which genotype is successful depends on the environment, in other words the effect of light, nutrition etc., but also parasites, predators etc. Biotechnology performs the trial and error process more efficiently, from a limited pool of starting material, and at the expense of fewer misfits.

– By means of technology, instruments are developed to make the earth hospitable and to keep it so, in the first place for people but, while not involving unnecessary suffering caused to people, also to other forms of life capable of suffering. The social acceptability of technology is a derivative of the risks which it entails. If the risks are predictable and controllable within reasonable margins, then there is nothing to bar the introduction of new technologies.

– With regard to physical planning, the integration is advocated of genetically modified crops in nature, in other words farmland. A controlled trial period must be observed. However, the safety regulations should not be overstated, because the risks are comparatively small-scale and local in nature, and they are in no way comparable with the genetic lottery of untamed nature.

– The scale enlargement entailed by the new world varieties need not be a problem as long as the global biodiversity is not affected by genetic erosion. This can be done by maintaining plots of wild nature, accompanied by the creation of gene banks. Modern cultivated crops already require an intensively controlled environment, and therefore are scarcely capable of invading wild nature; that applies all the more for deliberately modified plants.

– Although Third World problems are a result of economic scale enlargement, measures designed to ensure equitable distribution should nevertheless be taken at the international political level, and it is only from that angle that ethics come into the picture; it is not feasible to put the economy or technology in the dock, because the only duty of economists and technologists is to implement choices arrived at on a collective basis.

B. *The Steward*

– Although the steward perceives nature from an anthropocentric perspective, there are definite limits. The steward has been entrusted with the use of nature, not with its consumption. This curbs the dominator's expansiveness. As a minimum, the steward will endorse a duty to care for organisms other than humans, quite apart from the extent to which they resemble humans in their capacity to suffer. The problem then lies in the relative ranking of the intrinsic values which are recognized. Genetic manipulation of plants in the service of man is permitted, but not for just any arbitrary reason. Human interests prevail over the vital interests of animals and plants, but vital interests prevail in turn above purely economic interests. This debate has been continuing for some time with regard to the use of animals for experimental purposes: which is permitted for the purpose of testing important medicines, but not for testing cosmetics. As a general rule, vital interests of animals and plants may not be sacrificed to economic interests unless they serve a "higher interest"; it is debatable from case to case what this higher interest means.

– Technology is not a neutral instrument that can be applied in a good or bad manner. With technology, an instrumental relationship towards nature is implicitly exported to the Third World. For that reason, a plea is made for "adapted technology", in other words, technology rooted in the local socio-economic context and adapted to a specific relationship between culture and nature. In this relationship, nature is not normative, but care has to be taken not to disrupt the organization of individual species and ecosystems as self-contained entities. If that nevertheless threatens, human interests must yield, or at any rate restraint is called for. The steward will demand restraint especially with regard to horizontal gene transfer, to ensure that Creation or nature is not wrenched out of joint. The integrity of Creation or of nature as it has become by itself in the evolutionary process, represents a great good to the steward.

– The conservative steward, in matters of physical planning, is in favour of functional separation of agriculture, urban development, recreation, industry. The progressive steward endeavours to reconcile and combine nature and useful space as far as possible. For the conservative steward, that means it is essential to designate nature reserves, where nature is left to itself. The progressive steward opts for "nature development" according to the ecological model. In principle, the steward is not opposed to humanization of nature provided it is done with due respect.

– The scale enlargement of agriculture and the concomitant universalization of crops is a matter for concern, especially the consequences for the Third World. Ethical considerations take precedence above economics and politics. Technological interventions must also be based on respect and receptivity for the limits which self-organization of life imposes on it. Mankind can only impose its order on nature within the constraints of a meeting – fully defined in terms of quality – between culture and nature. Scale enlargement may not lead to the levelling of natural differences in the landscape.

C. The Partner

– The partner looks on life forms other than man as potential allies. This presupposes animals and plants having their own input in the interaction with humans. Nature is conceived of as an interplay of different life forms, in which each life form invests its own expressiveness and its intrinsic value. Such a conception of nature needs not in itself conflict with the scientific approach. It does demand a respectful relationship with nature. In this vision, mankind distinguishes itself from other life forms in that it not only participates biologically in nature but, in addition, has a relationship with nature. Because man therefore does not totally correlate to his biological origin, he may choose to belong to nature in an even more embracing sense than biologically alone. That freedom is expressed in an ethical attitude, in this case a self-chosen partnership with the concomitant respect for the other life forms. The partnership will generally be asymmetrical, because it consists of an interaction between life forms at different levels of organic complexity. Ecological farming in particular (as distinguished from the more cosmologically inspired biodynamic agriculture, which is to be classed in the participation attitude) satisfies these requirements.

– Mankind may exploit nature, so understood, by means of technological designs and interventions up to a certain extent, as long as it does not involve unnatural forcing of the life forms involved. Such exploitation may even be of mutual benefit. In such a "natural enterprise", however, in some cases human interests will have to yield to animal or vegetable interests. That decision may be made for example on the basis of the question as to whether, within the human framework concerned, the species-specific development of the life form concerned is beneficially or adversely affected. Such an assessment imposes limits on technological intervention in nature. Respect for natural equilibria is the norm here. By this route we arrive at the notion of "sustainable technology", that is to say, in the inorganic sector resource chain man-

agement (closing the substance cycles) and, also in biotechnology, techniques which operate within the margins of the self-regenerative capacity of nature.
– The form of physical planning demanded by partnership depends on whether the metaphor of partnership is interpreted in a strong or weak sense. Conservative partners share the tasks and allow one another scope for themselves on those matters where agreement is not yet possible, in other words conflicts are avoided, cooperation takes place where possible and separation where necessary, all in the interest of harmony. Progressive partners, on the other hand, see conflict rather as a constructive mode of relationship or as an opportunity for mutual growth: integration is pursued intensively. The former case exemplifies an approach to the physical area which yields functions separated by buffers, the latter case exemplifies optimized interwovenness, where necessary with the application of transitional zoning. Extrapolated into biotechnology, the genetically modified crops admitted sparingly by the partner could also be introduced in buffered form, or integrated in a zoning system, at any rate until their innocuity in the free field has been effectively proven.
– Scale enlargement may not degenerate into extensively monocultures, because that destroys the interaction between mutually supportive life forms. In agriculture, just as in human society, pluriformity is appreciated. "Biodiversity" – in a mutual interdependence of life forms – is the key word.
– The Third World problems can only be solved by means of solidarity coupled with variety. Developing countries are given rights to their natural gene pool. The traditional cultivation techniques must be protected. Genetic modification performed on traditionally managed plants still remains accountable to the original managers.

D. The Participant
– For the participant, nature represents the totality of interdependent and interwoven life forms. Mankind is an integral part of this nature. For that reason respect is owed to the various life forms, not only because of the intrinsic value of other organisms, but also because of the complexity of nature: the countless relationships between organisms have a surplus value that exceeds their usefulness to mankind. From the interplay between life forms in natural balances, the participant draws more far-reaching consequences than the partner. He makes a number of principled choices in order to set limits on man's intervention in nature. Although the participant must also inevitably intervene in nature for the purpose of food production, in doing so he never-

theless endeavours as far as possible to make use of the inherent dynamism of natural processes. Biodynamic agriculture is an attempt to give shape to this approach on the basis of a spiritual vision of the relationship between man and nature.

– In the case of the participant, science and technology are based on a holistic approach. Participation and high technology are not necessarily incompatible with one another. For example, the participant will support the growing of crops for non-food uses, that is to say energy production from vegetable materials. The central principle is that technology should guide rather than force the processes taking place in the soil and in the crop. A moderate use of finite energy resources is a precondition. Technology remains subject to local self-sufficiency in energy and to support by agriculture for natural self-regulation.

– In his approach to physical planning, the participant tries to follow the natural scheme of things as closely as possible. Cultural interventions in nature for farming or housing purposes must create optimized conditions permitting nature to develop itself. Scale enlargement (for example, by means of land reform) is objectionable because it forces nature to observe economically profitable production methods; in that case, the machinery employed threatens to be the factor determining the size of plots. Cultivation techniques are biological in nature. Diseases, pests and weeds form part of the natural balance; they can be counteracted for example by matching suitable crops together. In agriculture, the participant makes use of biological and physical cultivation measures to ensure the quality and quantity of the harvest, without introducing alien and disruptive elements such as agricultural chemicals into the environment. In this context, biotechnological developments are followed very critically, and they will be applied only very incidentally for the present.

– Agriculture and the food industry both feature their own optimal scale. Global industrial networks and matching transport systems are both energy-intensive and inefficient. Smallness of scale is the standard. It is associated with a preference for the food in season and from the region.

– Third World problems must be addressed on an integrated basis by means of economic and social reforms, both in the North and South, if a sustainable society is indeed to emerge. Changes in that direction may be expected in part from Western subcultures which adopt a position of solidarity with cultural minorities in the Third World. This review of fundamental attitudes now enables us to practise reasoning on the basis of fundamental attitudes relating to specific ethical problems.

VI Ethical Evaluation Based on Fundamental Attitudes

At the present state of development, the ethical evaluations which are neces-sary with regard to specific applications of biotechnology relate a number of topical problem areas. These have been tabulated and subjected to ethical evaluation on the basis of each fundamental attitude.

In accordance with the custom that has become accepted in this debate, the possible options are formulated as follows: "No" – "no, unless" – "yes, pro-vided that" – "yes". In the case "no, unless" and "yes, provided that" the bur-den of proof is reversed: in the case of "no, unless", the burden of proof rests with the person desiring change, in the case of "yes, provided that" it rests with the opponent. In this case, "no, unless" means that the person wishing to make genetic modifications must present good reasons for departing from the prevailing "no". "Yes, provided that" means that the person wishing to object to genetic modification, which in principle has been accepted, must demonstrate that nevertheless generally accepted values are violated or that harmful consequences may occur, and that these must subsequently be item-ized under the "provided that" clause. Hitherto, such a formulation of ethical judgements has only been made in the assessment framework drawn up by the Schroten Committee for biotechnology in animals. The principle of "no, unless" has been politically ratified with regard to biotechnology in animals.

According to conventional anthropocentric moral, biotechnology with regard to plants would qualify for "yes, provided that". In his process of eval-uation relating to biotechnology, the anthropocentrist observes the principle that the more remote from man the life forms concerned are, the more is per-mitted. Such reasoning results a priori in the following priorities: biotechnol-ogy in humans "no", or very exceptionally (gene therapy); in animals "no, unless", in plants "yes, provided that", in bacteria "yes" (subject to the neces-sary precautionary measures). Because it is precisely the exclusively anthro-pocentric point of view that is being considered in the present report, further differentiations are applied in the ethical evaluation. In the first place, the "no", "no, unless", "yes, provided that" or "yes" is not determined in a gener-al way for all biotechnology in plants, but a differentiation is made between different applications and, secondly, the various problem cases are assessed differently according to fundamental attitude.

Table of differentiated ethical evaluations of genetic modification

	Dominator	Steward	Partner	Participant
A. Herbicide-resistant crops	Yes	Yes,	No, unless provided that	No
B. Disease-resistant crops (biotic stress)	Yes	Yes	Yes,	No, unless provided that
C. Abiotic stress-resistant crops (cold, drought, salt tolerance)	Yes	Yes	Yes,	No, unless provided that
D. Aesthetic change (shape, colour, smell, taste)	Yes	No, unless provided that	No	No
E. Introduction of alien elements	Yes	No, unless provided that	No	No
F. (Economic) protection by patenting	Yes	No, unless provided that	No	No
G. (Economic) protection by breeders' rights	Yes	Yes	Yes,	No, unless provided that

The table contains a diagrammatic presentation of the morally ranked order within the fundamental attitudes for seven separate problem areas in the field of genetic modification of crops. In order to demonstrate how a specific ethical evaluation is ultimately formulated, a brief justification is given for each of the choices made. This is followed by a number of comments regarding the interpretation and scope of the model. The table serves merely as an example and not as a definitive assessment framework. The table presents the findings of a preliminary ethical evaluation. The present report does not claim to cut any Gordian knots for others, but rather should be seen as an invitation to all concerned to arrange matters in systematic order by means of the fundamental attitude approach. The report is an invitation to ethical debate, and is not intended to have any policing function.

A. Herbicide-resistant crops

The *dominator* regards any weed present in cultivation as an undesired evil. By definition weeds do not belong in cultivation, and their presence is always at the expense of the cultivated crop. For that reason, they can be combated, and the necessary use of herbicides for this purpose is permitted. Herbicide-resistant crops permit a reduction in the use of herbicides, and they furthermore result in an ongoing improvement in cultivation (higher yields).

The *steward* applies the criterion that weeds should not have an adverse effect on the yield and quality of the crops, but he seeks alternatives to herbicides. He is therefore interested in mechanical weed control. He monitors the results of research, and wherever possible he applies the techniques on his own farm. At any rate, a selective use of herbicides is advocated. Herbicide-resistant crops can be employed provided they do not cause any ecological damage.

The *partner* proceeds on the principle that weeds are inevitable when cultivating crops, and in fact they are also an associated element. The aim of cultivation is to achieve balance and control of the weed population. Herbicide-resistant varieties could play a role in weed control, but in this field biotechnology definitely has no priority.

The *participant* views weeds as an integral part of the overall agro-ecosystem. Weeds reflect soil conditions, and thereby give a signal to agriculture. A combination of cultivation measures (choice of suitable variety and crop, soil management, rapid ground cover and mechanical weed control) are required to suppress the level of weeds on the plots and enable a good harvest to be achieved. Herbicides are not used.

Herbicide-resistant varieties therefore have no significance for the participant.

B. Disease-resistant crops

The development of disease-resistant crops provides an answer to biotic stress originating from viruses, fungi and insects.

The *dominator* considers diseases alien to the cultivation system. Diseases occur at the expense of yield and quality of the cultivated crop, and therefore they can be combated. Disease-resistant crops are a means to this end, and until now they are indeed the only solution for virus diseases.

The *steward* agrees with this view. Diseases and pests affect the crops and therefore they have to be combated. Disease-resistant crops are an important aid in the necessary control measures, because they are environmentally friendly.

The *partner* knows that diseases are not completely unavoidable, but that they must be maintained at the lowest possible controllable level. Control measures should only be taken where damage thresholds are exceeded, and even then with the smallest possible use of pesticides. The approach is based on the principle of natural balances; biological methods are therefore to be preferred. Chemical pesticides must be avoided as far as possible. Disease-resistant crops automatically represent an improvement. There is a potential role for biotechnology here.

The *participant* does not use any chemical/synthetic pesticides. Diseases are regarded as an expression of an imbalance in cultivation conditions. Attempts are made by means of an appropriate choice of cultivation system and a combination of cultivation measures to keep diseases and pests under control. Disease-resistant varieties may form part of preventive measures, but they are never an end in themselves. Biotechnologically developed varieties are not rejected out of hand, but they are analysed critically by the participant in view of the reductionist method.

C. Abiotic stress-resistant crops

The *dominator* regards abiotic stress as a handicap that can and must be conquered. Stress-resistant crops also enable cultivation to be carried out under less favourable external conditions.

The *steward* agrees with this. Stress-resistant crops also enable land of lesser quality to be brought into cultivation, which has a yield-raising effect and contributes towards the food supply.

The *partner* believes that abiotic stress-resistant crops may offer a solution in certain cases, but that it is nevertheless necessary to assess whether they do not lead to undesired side-effects. This is because new crops can be introduced into environments which were previously unable to support them, with all the resultant possible shifts in ecosystems that entails.

The *participant* considers abiotic stress-resistant crops to be a superfluous development, because the participant employs regionally and climatically adapted crops as a matter of principle. At the very most, abiotic stress-resistant crops might be considered if they were able to eliminate major bottlenecks in the traditional cultivation system, but within the cultivation system it is primarily the cultivation measures that are adapted in order to overcome problems.

D. Aesthetic change (shape, colour, smell, flavour)

The *dominator* considers morphological change to be an enrichment of the arsenal of opportunities and a source of new commercial opportunities. The market will determine which developments are successful and which are not.

The *steward* does not share this optimism. Introducing aesthetic changes is only meaningful if it serves a precisely defined higher value than economic value alone. Concern for what exists leads the steward to observe a policy of restraint.

The *partner* considers the pursuit of aesthetic change as a non-meaningful development. The end is out of all proportion to the concomitant intervention in the natural abundance of species. Nature contains sufficient variation to guarantee a sufficiently wide supply.

The *participant* agrees with the partner. Aesthetic changes by means of biotechnology are unnecessary and incompatible with the philosophy of the cultivation method.

E. Introduction of alien elements

The *dominator* considers that it is permissible to introduce alien genetic information with the objective of creating new elements in plants.

The *steward* feels that this permissive attitude is going too far. In this case, commercial considerations should not be the deciding factor. Convincing evidence must be furnished that the crop cannot be produced in a different way and that no practicable alternatives are available. This might apply, for example, in the case of the manufacture of unique medicines.

Both the *partner* and the *participant* reject this development. In their view, the plant's intrinsic value is intolerably violated by the introduction of alien elements (in the case of the manufacture of pharmaceuticals, an exception may sometimes be possible).

F. (Economic) protection by means of patent rights

The *dominator* considers patent rights to be an appropriate means for promoting the necessarily (bio)technological innovation and of providing the entrepreneur with an adequate reward for his efforts, which are of benefit to society. Particularly with regard to plants, that presents no insurmountable problems.

The *steward* finds it difficult to accept patent rights in the case of living organisms, including plants. The responsibility for their care is not readily compatible with the principle of patent rights which provides the entrepreneur with exclusive rights for a certain time period. The steward can approve a patent on genes isolated under laboratory conditions, but patents on higher life forms such as plants are not permitted.

The *partner* rejects patents on living organisms and even on vital building-blocks. The principle of patent rights is not compatible with the recognized intrinsic value of life forms.

The *participant* agrees with this. Patent rights perceived in the form of a claim are a human construction imposed on nature from the outside, and is therefore at odds with the notion that nature itself should direct the cultivation method. What is more, products originating from nature, including varieties, should be freely available to everybody. The participant has a high regard for the farmer's privilege.

G. (Economic) protection by means of breeder's rights

The *dominator* has absolutely no problem with breeder's rights. And in fact he usually regards them as being insufficient. The dominator prefers patent rights, which provide still better protection.

The *steward* is perfectly satisfied with breeder's rights. These rights meet the wish for a measure of protection for the holder of the breeder's rights, which fosters the responsible exploitation of varieties.

The *partner* has far fewer problems with breeder's rights than with patent rights. On condition that new varieties can be integrated into nature in a responsible way, the partner does not object to the operation of breeder's rights.

The *participant* has less problems with breeder's rights than with patent rights. Rights represent a reward for the efforts of the plant breeder. However, breeders' rights or the like can never be claimed on properties.

The varieties must be available to everybody (also in the economic sense) and farmers must be allowed to propagate their own crop seeds.

Finally, the following comments may help to improve the readability of the table:

1. The "yes" and "no" columns may differ appreciably between the techniques to achieve the desired aim – for example, "herbicide resistance". A table for "classical" breeding will be filled in differently. In the problem areas "aesthetic change" and "introduction of alien elements", for example, both the dominator's and the steward's attitude towards classical breeding will be "yes", whereas the partner and participant will reply a qualified "yes, provided that". They make a reservation with regard to the technology employed because physical and/or chemical techniques used in order to make the "classical" cross may be perceived as so alien to nature that such a technique is to be rejected. An example of this is mutagenesis. Such a differentiation in technique employed has not been applied for each problem field in this case.

2. The distribution of "yes" and "no" replies, with or without further qualification, over the matrix of fundamental attitudes and problem areas is no more than a snapshot. The table is not intended to be a blueprint for an assessment on the basis of which certain developments are banned and other developments are approved for an extended period of investment. In contrast, the table presents an example of ethical evaluation. This approach agrees with the changing role of government. While business and industry has for the past decade been confronted with a complex system of licences, levies and sanctions, now a facilitating policy is being pursued, supplementing existing regulations. In this way, business and industry are invited – in consultation with other players involved such as consumer organizations – to help in defining the standards and, if necessary, placing constraints up on itself (social self-regulation), which can subsequently be legislated. The present report is intended to assist communication between government and industry on ethical matters, and therefore it does not contain any subscriptions.

3. The fundamental attitudes have been charted in accordance with a typically ideal classification along a spectrum ranging from anthropocentrism to ecocentrism. The consistency of actual positions adopted within society can be assessed by comparing them with the given model. But this may also reveal discrepancies, in particular for "stewardship". Viewed historically, steward-

ship has been articulated in a Protestant denominational matrix, and it has indeed entered Dutch politics as such. The typically ideal stewardship as presented here should of course not depart unduly from its historical form, but on the other hand it does not automatically coincide. This is because the freedom must be ensured to choose a given fundamental attitude without being forced to embrace a given political party as a result. Nevertheless, a choice of fundamental attitude can never be made without commitment, because it definitely involves normative orientations with deep moral implications.

4. Although the various fundamental attitudes are not assigned norms in a comparative way, for example in the sense that stewardship or partnership is a priori "better" or "more justifiable" than the other attitudes, from the social point of view a gradual shift can nevertheless be observed towards a more ecocentric approach. Each of the fundamental attitudes sets its own criteria for justifiable actions by man towards other life forms, but the attitude in which man claims exclusive control of nature is beginning to lose its social base. Government policy, also, is beginning to take increasing account of nature as a value in itself, that is to say quite apart from its functions on behalf of mankind. Although it is not possible to express an a priori preference for any one fundamental attitude, at the present moment – at this spot in Europe – a growing political base appears to be developing in favour of stewardship at least, if not partnership. Of course, normative guidelines cannot be derived from actual developments. The fact of existence cannot be construed as implying justification. Ethics does not move with fashion. However, recent technological developments do reveal some ethical embarrassment. Now that we are capable of modifying life itself at the genetic level, our generally accepted ethical code relating to life proves to be no longer adequate. Unprecedented techniques force us to revise our existing scale of values, and to redefine our principles in such a way as to assign an independent ethical status to nature. That may require us to abdicate our throne in nature and shift our fundamental attitude accordingly.

5. To the extent that fundamental attitudes are borne collectively, they shift gradually over time, but that shift is linked to a certain level of prosperity. According to the Brundtland Report, the developing countries must first be allowed to catch up economically before they may be expected to assign a high priority to environmental concern. That explains the linkage between inhibited economic growth and sustainability in the Brundtland report. Extrapolated to fundamental attitudes, this would mean that for the time being the shift towards ecocentrism in Third World countries will not take

place at the same rate as in the wealthy countries. However, this representation conceals a Western prejudice. The introduction of economic competition in traditional cultures may actually cause a break with an existing partnership with nature. That may perhaps be prevented if the West is prepared to compensate the developing countries for the genetic diversity which it removes from the countries concerned. In that case, a catch-up manoeuvre on the part of the developing countries could take place with less expense to the solidarity between man and nature that may still exist there. Our own demonstrable shift in fundamental attitudes commits us not only to nature but also to our fellow men in the Third World, including their relationship to nature.

VII Conclusions and Recommendations

– An ethical evaluation of the application of genetic modification in plants cannot be confined to an assessment of extrinsic consequences on the basis of risk analyses, but it also demands – at an even earlier stage – substantive definitions of position relating to the intrinsic value of nature. In that respect, aspects such as images of nature play an important role.
– The present report offers an inventory of "fundamental attitudes", that is to say "orientations of basic values", which can be used for the purpose of making an ethical evaluation from case to case. The line of ethical reasoning differs in the various fundamental attitudes. As an example of such ethical assessment, the report contains a table showing a position definition based on each of the various fundamental attitudes with reference to a number of problem areas in plant biotechnology.
– The process of ethical evaluation relating to innovative technologies will never be complete. If the government advocates a facilitating policy, it must open up an ongoing dialogue. It is therefore recommended that the ethical debate be placed on an institutionalized footing, not by appointing an ad-hoc Review Committee but by – in the context of social self-regulation – appointing a committee which, as biotechnological developments take place, prepares proposals for appropriate (self-)limitation. The necessary ethical evaluation can then take place in a discussion between representatives of the various fundamental attitudes recruited from governmental organizations, trade and industry, and other organizations concerned. In order to maintain the

debate, the set of ethical terms must, by means of continued research, be developed further than was possible in this report.

– In this report the fundamental attitudes are not themselves assessed for ethical content. Each of them independently represents a consistent ethical starting-point. Nevertheless, new technological developments require us to define our position as to the degree in which we wish to honour natural values, which may mean a shift in the dominant fundamental attitude. Politicians will have to consider whether the dominant anthropocentric way of thinking, which regards nature as being merely functionally related to human comfort, must be required in the light of sustainable development to make way for a more nature-oriented (ecocentric) position. Based on ethical debate with new standards, the political world can initiate such a gradual shift (or respond to it).

– New technological developments cannot be legitimized by pleading for continuation of an already accepted approach if that approach requires re-evaluation on the basis of the new developments. Mutagenesis and transgenesis are unprecedented and even in nature highly exceptional or totally absent (certainly in the case of horizontal gene transfer). It is therefore to be recommended that these techniques will be applied only with great caution.

– Although it is an ambivalent term, "sustainable development" is nevertheless capable of providing a yardstick for the application of biotechnology in agriculture. Measured by that criterion, large-scale applications requiring a global market must yield to applications which optimize the relationship between crop and the environment at the local level. Developing countries will be able to benefit if they also acquire legally and economically protected control of the biodiversity and the gene pool present there.

Bibliography

1. Roger Straughan, 1992, "Ethics, Morality and Crop Biotechnology", ICI Seeds, Reading University.
2. Cf.: Roderick Nash, 1989, "The rights of nature: a history of environmental ethics", University of Wisconsin Press.
3. Jaap van der Wal and Edith Lammerts van Bueren, 1993, "Zit er toekomst in ons DNA", (Does our DNA hold a future?, in the Dutch Working Group on Genetic Engineering and Judgment Formation, Driebergen).
4. For a hermeneutic approach to the problem, see also: Günter Altner, 1992, "Gutachten: Ethische Aspekte der gentechnischen Veränderungen von Pflanzen, Wissenschaftszentrum Berlin für Sozialforschung".

5. Wim Zweers, 1989, "Houdingen ten opzichte van de natuur", (attitudes towards nature) (in Dutch), in: Heidemij tijdschrift, Vol. 100, No. 3, pp. 774-80. For a more recent vision, see W. Zweers, 1995, "Participeren aan de natuur", Uitgeverij Jan van Arkel, Utrecht.

APPENDIX 2

Literature on Environmental Philosophy and Some Related Subjects

Wim Zweers

The following list is based mainly on the bibliography of my book *Participeren aan de natuur*, mentioned below in the section on Ecological world-view. However, in the interest of the subject of the present volume, many titles have been omitted and others have been added (mostly those I am personally acquainted with), with an emphasis on Dutch contributions. The list is by no means comprehensive: it is intended as a rough and introductory guide to *some* of the literature on the subject only. Titles are in the original language. Where I have abridged references to readers etc., unless otherwise indicated, full information can be found in the first section: environmental philosophy.

Contents:

- Environmental philosophy and ethics: general
- Journals
- Aesthetics, Landscape, Art
- Agricultural practice (with respect to spirituality)
- Animal-man relationships
- Anthropology, philosophical (incl. hermeneutics)
- Attitudes towards nature (incl. paradigms)
- Biology
- Deep Ecology
- Developing countries
- Ecofeminism
- Ecological world view (incl. "Gaia")
- Ecological and Environmental Science
- History
- Intrinsic value
- Marxism
- Non-western cultures
- Physics
- Policy, Politics, Democracy
- Social and economic philosophy
- Spirituality, Ecological experience
- Technology
- Theology, Religion
- Miscellaneous

Environmental philosophy and ethics: general

(Anonymous), Groene filosofie en groene politiek, spec. issue of *Krisis*, september 1984.

(Anonymous), Milieufilosofie, spec. issue of *Wijsgerig Perspectief op Maatschappij en Wetenschap*, vol. 34 no. 6, 1993/94.

Achterberg, W., Op zoek naar een ecologische ethiek, in: W. Achterberg en W. Zweers (red.) 1984, p. 142-171.

Achterberg, W., Gronden van moreel respect voor de natuur, in: W. Achterberg en W. Zweers (red.) 1986, p. 105-135.

Achterberg, W., *Partners in de natuur; een onderzoek naar de aard en de fundamenten van een ecologische ethiek*, Uitgeverij Jan van Arkel, Utrecht, 1986.

Achterberg, W., *Humanisme zonder arrogantie; Modern humanisme en ecocentrisme*, Oratie Landbouwuniversiteit, Wageningen, 1992.

Achterberg, W., Milieucrisis en humanisme; Varianten van ecologisch humanisme, in: P. B. Cliteur en D. J. van Houten (red.), *Humanisme; Theorie en Praktijk*, De Tijdstroom, Utrecht, 1993, p. 436-447.

Achterberg, W., *Samenleving, natuur en duurzaamheid: Een inleiding in de milieufilosofie*, Van Gorcum, Assen, 1994.

Achterberg, W. (red.), *Natuur: uitbuiting of respect*, Kok/Agora, Kampen, 1989.

Achterberg, W., en W. Zweers (red.), *Milieucrisis en Filosofie; Westers bewustzijn en vervreemde natuur*, Ekologische Uitgeverij, Amsterdam, 1984.

Achterberg, W., en W. Zweers (red.), *Milieufilosofie tussen theorie en praktijk; van ecologisch perspectief naar maatschappelijke toepassing*, Uitgeverij Jan van Arkel, Utrecht, 1986.

Achterhuis, H., *Van moeder aarde tot ruimteschip; Humanisme en milieucrisis*, Oratie Landbouwuniversiteit, Wageningen, 1990.

Attfield, R., *The ethics of Environmental Concern*, Blackwell, Oxford, 1982.

Barbour, I. G. (Ed.), *Western Man and Environmental Ethics*, Addison-Wesly, Reading, 1973.

Barbour, I. G., *Technology, environment and human values*, Praeger, New-York, 1980.

Birnbacher, D., (Hrsg.), *Oekologie und Ethik*, Reclam, Stuttgart, 1980.

Birnbacher, D., *Verantwortung für zukünftige Generationen*, Reclam, Stuttgart, 1988.

Blackstone, W.T. (Ed.), *Philosophy and the Environmental Crisis*, University of Georgia Press, Athens, 1974.

Brennan, A., *Thinking About Nature; an Investigation of Nature, Value and Ecology*, Routledge, London, 1988.

Brennan, A., *Environmental Philosophy, An Introductory Survey*, Univ. of St. Andrews, Centre for Philosophy and Public Affairs, 1990.

Callicott, J. Baird, *In Defense of the Land Ethic; Essays in Environmental Philosophy*, State University of New-York Press, Albany, 1989.

Disch, R. (Ed.), *The Ecological Conscience*, Prentice-Hall, Englewood Cliffs, 1970.

Ehrenfeld, D., *The Arrogance of Humanism*, Oxford University Press, Oxford, 1981.

Elliott, R., and A. Gare, *Environmental Philosophy*, Pennsylvania State University Press, University Park, 1983.

Evernden, N., *The Natural Alien; Humankind and Environment*, Univ. of Toronto Press, Toronto, 1985.

Hargrove, E., *Foundations of Environmental Ethics*, Prentice-Hall, Englewood Cliffs, 1989.

Kohak, E., *The Embers and the Stars; A philosophical inquiry into the moral sense of nature*, Univ. of Chicago Press, 1984.

Koppen, K. v., e. a. (red.), *Natuur en mens; Visies op natuurbeheer vanuit wetenschap, levensbeschouwing en politiek*, Pudoc, Wageningen, 1984.

List, P. C. (Ed.), *Radical Environmentalism; Philosophy and Tactics*, Wadsworth Publ. Comp., Belmont, 1993.

Mannison, D., a. o. (Eds.), *Environmental Philosophy*, Australian National University, Department of Philosophy, 1980.

Merchant, C., *Radical Ecology; the Search for a Livable World*, Routledge, London, 1992.

Meyer-Abich, K., *Aufstand für die Natur; Von der Umwelt zur Mitwelt*, Hanser, München, 1990.

Meyer-Abich, K. (Hrsg.), *Frieden mit der Natur*, Herder, Freiburg, 1979.

Passmore, J., *Man's Responsibility for Nature*, London, Duckworth, 1980 (1974).

Rolston, H., *Philosophy Gone Wild; Essays in Environmental Ethics*, Prometheus Books, New-York, 1986.

Rolston, H., *Environmental Ethics; Duties to and Values in the Natural World*, Temple University Press, Philadelphia, 1988.

Scherer, D. and T. Attig (Eds.), *Ethics and the environment*, Prentice-Hall, Englewood Cliffs, 1983.

Schultz, R., and J. Hughes (Eds.), *Ecological Consciousness; Essays from the Earthday X Colloquium*, University Press of America, Washington, 1981.

Shrader-Frechette, K. S., *Environmental Ethics*, Boxwood Press, Pacific Grove, 1981.

Sylvan, R., and D. Bennett, *The Greening of Ethics; From Human Chauvinism to Deep-Green Theory*, White Horse Press/Univ. of Arizona Press, Cambridge, UK/Tucson, USA, 1994.

Taylor, P., *Respect for Nature; a theory of environmental ethics*, Princeton University Press, Princeton, 1986.

Vermeersch, E., *De ogen van de panda; een milieufilosofisch essay*, Marc van de Wiele, Brugge, 1988.

Vermeersch, E., De toekomst van de milieufilosofie, in: W. Zweers (red.) 1991, p. 255-268.

Wal, G. A., van der, Het milieu: een voorgeprogrammeerd probleem?, in: G. A. van der Wal en R. M. Hogendoorn (red.) 1993, p. 65-81.

Wal, G. A. van der, en R. M. Hogendoorn (red.), *Natuur of Milieu; Filosofische overwegingen bij milieu en beleid*, Erasmus Universiteit, Faculteit Wijsbegeerte, Rotterdam, 1993.

Zimmerman, M. E., a. o. (Eds.), *Environmental Philosophy; From Animal Rights to Radical Ecology*, Prentice-Hall, Englewood Cliffs, 1993.

Zweers, W., Milieufilosofie, een inleidende oriëntatie, in: W. Achterberg en W. Zweers (red.) 1984, p. 7-24.

Zweers, W., Milieufilosofie, een overzicht van standpunten en literatuur, in: *Filosofie en Praktijk*, vol. 8 no. 4, dec. 1987, p. 180-205.

Zweers, W., Een kader voor de milieufilosofie, in: W. Zweers (red.) 1991, p. 9-25.

Zweers, W., Milieufilosofie, in: J. J. Boersema e. a. (red.), *Basisboek Milieukunde*, Boom, Meppel, 1991, 4e druk, hfd. 18.

Zweers, W., Waartoe milieufilosofie?, in: *Filosofie en Praktijk*, vol. 13 no. 1, maart 1992, p. 20-27.

Zweers, W. (red.), *Op zoek naar een ecologische cultuur; Milieufilosofie in de jaren '90*, Ambo, Baarn, 1991 (also in English: W. Zweers en J.J. Boersema (Eds.), *Ecology, Technology and Culture; Essays in Environmental Philosophy*, The White Horse Press, Cambridge, 1994).

Zweers, W., en W. T. de Groot, Milieufilosofie en milieukunde, een relatie in wording, in: *Milieu; Tijdschrift voor Milieukunde*, vol. 2, 1987 no. 5, p. 145-150.

Journals

Environmental Ethics; an interdisciplinary journal dedicated to the philosophical aspects of environmental problems, Center for Environmental Philosophy/Univ. of North Texas, Quarterly, $20, 1994= vol. 16.

Environmental Values, The White Horse Press, Cambridge, Quarterly, $60, 1994= vol. 3.

The Trumpeter; Journal of Ecosophy, Lightstar Press, Victoria, Canada, Quarterly, $25, 1994= vol. 11.

Newsletter Int. Society for Environmental Ethics, (Netherlands: W. Achterberg, Fac. of Philosophy, Univ. of Amsterdam), Quarterly, $10, 1994= vol. 5.

Aesthetics, Landscape, Art

(Anonymous), *Berg Beeld, een onderzoek naar relaties tussen kunst en landschap*, Jan van Eyck Akademie, Maastricht, 1990/Rijksgeologische Dienst, 1991 (incl. P. Kockelkoren: De betekenis van het landschap in postmoderne tijden).

(Anonymous), *Landschaft*, Konkursbuch 18, Gehrke Verlag, Tübingen, 1987.

(Anonymous), Landschapsbeeld en landschapsontwerp, spec. issue of *Landschap, Tijdschrift voor landschapsecologie en milieukunde*, vol. 1 no. 1, 1984.

Austin, R. C., Beauty: A Foundation for Environmental Ethics, in: *Environmental Ethics*, vol. 7 no. 3, Fall 1985, p. 197-209.

Berleant, A., Aesthetic Perception in Environmental Design, in: Nasar (Ed.) 1988 (see below), p. 84-98.

Berleant, A., *The Aesthetics of Environment*, Temple University Press, Philadelphia, 1992.

Böhme, G., *Für eine ökologische Naturästhetik*, Ed. Suhrkamp NF 556, Frankfurt am Main, 1989.

Böhme, G., Naturästhetik, in: *Natürlich Natur; Über Natur im Zeitalter ihrer technischen Reproduzierbarkeit*, Ed. Suhrkamp, NF 680, Frankfurt am Main, 1992, p. 107-181.

Carlson, A., Nature and positive aesthetics, in: *Environmental Ethics*, vol. 6 no. 1, Spring 1984, p. 5-35.

Chaloupka, W., John Dewey's Social Aesthetics as a Precedent for Environmental Thought, in: *Environmental Ethics*, vol. 9 no. 3, Fall 1987, p. 243-261.

Coleman, E. J., Is nature ever unaesthetic?, in: *Between the Species*, vol. 5 no. 3, Summer 1989, p. 138-147.

Gablik, S., *The Reenchantment of Art*, Thames and Hudson, London, 1991.

Groh, R. und D., Von den schrecklichen zu den erhabenen Bergen. Zur Entstehung ästhetischer Naturerfahrung, in: (id.) *Weltbild und Naturaneigung; zur Kulturgeschichte der Natur*, Suhrkamp, Frankfurt am Main, 1991, p. 92-150.

Hepburn, R. W., Contemporary Aesthetics and the Neglect of Natural Beauty, in: B. Williams and A. Montefiore (Eds.), *British Analytical Philosophy*, Routledge, London, 1966, p. 285-311.

Hoog, S. de, *Aangeharkt Nederland; beschouwingen over het landschap van de verzorgingsstaat*, Anthos, Baarn, 1984.

Kemal, S., and I. Gaskell (Eds.), *Landscape, Natural Beauty and the Arts*, Cambridge Univ. Press, 1993.

Kockelkoren, P., De vernieuwing van Nederland, in: *Vormgeven aan Natuurontwikkeling*, App. to Blauwe Kamer/Profiel, april 1993, Stichting Locus, p. 10-16.

Kockelkoren, P. Filosofie van de dijkverzwaring, in: *Filosofie en Praktijk*, vol. 15 no. 1, voorjaar 1994, p. 1-16.

Lemaire. T., *Filosofie van het landschap*, Ambo, Baarn, 1970.

Lippe, R. zur, *Sinnenbewusztsein; Grundlegung einer anthropologischen Ästhetik*, Rowohlt, Reinbek, 1987.

Lörzing, H., *De angst voor het nieuwe landschap; beschouwingen over landschapsontwerp en landschapsbeheer*, Staatsuitgeverij, Den Haag, 1982.

Nasar, J. L., (Ed.), *Environmental Aesthetics*, Cambridge University Press, Cambridge, 1988.

Noack, H., Das naturschöne als Motiv des Umweltschutzes und der Beitrag des ästhetischen Sinns zur Wahrnehmung der Natur, in: K. M. Meyer-Abich (Hrsg.), 1979, p. 59-75.

Röhring, K., Der heilende Blick – Von der Befähigung, die ökologische Partitur des Planeten zu lesen, in: K. Meyer-Abich (Hrsg.) 1979, p. 39-59.

Schneider, G., *Naturschönheit und Kritik; Zur Aktualität von Kants Kritik der Urteilskraft für die Umwelterziehung*, Königshausen und Neumann, Würzburg, 1994.

Schweizer, H. R., *Vom ursprünglichen Sinn der Aesthetik*, Verlag Rudolf Kugler, Oberwil-Zug, 1976.

Schweizer, H. R., und A. Wildermuth (Hrsg.), *Die Entdeckung der Phänomene; Dokumente einer Philosophie der sinnlichen Erkenntnis*, Schwabe, Basel, 1981.

Seel, M., *Eine Aesthetik der Natur*, Suhrkamp, Frankfurt am Main, 1991.

Sepänmaa, Y., *The Beauty of the Environment; A general model for environmental aesthetics*, Helsinki, Suomalainen Tiedeakatemia, 1986 (2nd. ed.: Env. Ethics Books, Univ. of North Texas, Denton).

Toorn, W. van, De vergeten stad, in: G. A. van der Wal en R. M. Hogendoorn (red.) 1993, p. 43-49.

Wessell, L. P., *Zur Funktion des Aesthetischen in der Kosmologie Alfred North Whiteheads*, Peter Lang, Frankfurt am Main, 1990.

Agricultural practice (with respect to spirituality) (information supplied by F. Verkleij)

Balfour, L., *The living soil and the Haughley experiment*, Faber and Faber, London, 1975.

Cuthberson, T., *Enchanted garden. Alan Chadwick's organic method of gardening*. Rider and Comp./Hutchinson, London, 1978.

Hodges, J., *Harvesting the suburbs. Australian backyard gardening – a natural approch*, Downs Printing Comp., Toowoomba, Queensland, 1985.

Howard, A., *An agricultural testament*, Oxford University Press, London/New-York, 1943.

Fukuoka, M., *The one-straw revolution*, Rodale Press, 1978.

Fukuoka, M., *The road back to nature; regaining the paradise lost*, Japan Publ., Tokyo/New-York, 1987.

Koepf, H., B., D. Petterson, W. Schaumann, *Biodynamic agriculture*, AnthroposophicPress, Spring Valley, New-York, 1976 (also in Dutch).

Mollison, B., *Permaculture: a practical guide for a sustainable future*, Island Press, Washington, 1990.

Small Wright, M., *Al het leven is goddelijk; Ekologie voor de Nieuwe Tijd*, Ankh-Hermes, Deventer, 1985.

Small Wright, M., *Perelandra Garden Workbook; A complete guide to gardening with nature intelligence*, Perelandra, Warrenton, Virginia, 1993.

Steiner, R., *Agriculture; A course of eight lectures*, Biodynamic Agricultural Association, London, 1974(3) also in Dutch: *De Landbouwcursus*).

Thompson, P. B., *Spirit of the Soil; Agriculture and Environmental Ethics*, Routledge, London, 1994.

Animal-man relationships

(Anonymous), Mensen en dieren, spec. issue of *Rekenschap*, vol. 37 no. 1, maart 1990.

Achterberg, W., Dierproeven en ethiek, in: *Filosofie en Praktijk*, vol. 10 no. 4, nov. 1989, p. 180-197.

Heeger, R., Mensen, dieren en principes; Over de ethische toetsing van proeven met dieren, in: *Filosofie en Praktijk*, vol. 9 no. 4, dec. 1988, p. 169-181.

Lijmbach, S., Dier of ding, in: *Filosofie en Praktijk*, vol. 10 no. 3, sept. 1989, p. 147-161.

Lijmbach, S., "De stier" van Potter en biggen die gecastreerd worden: over de onmogelijkheid van een hermeneutische natuurwetenschap, in: W. Zweers (red.) 1991, p. 119-127.

Noske, B., Zijn dieren groen? De milieubeweging tussen anthropocentrisme en biologisme, in: Krisis, sept. 1984, p. 5-16.

Noske, B., *Huilen met de wolven; Een interdisciplinaire benadering van de mens-dier relatie*, Van Gennep, Amsterdam, 1988 (also in English).

Regan, T., *The Case for Animal Rights*, Routledge, London, 1984.

Singer, P., *Animal Liberation; a new ethics for our treatment of animals*, Random House, New-York, 1975.

Verhoog, H., Genetische manipulatie van dieren, in: *Filosofie en Praktijk*, vol. 12 no. 2, juni 1991, p. 87-107.

Vorstenbosch, J., en N. Endenburg, Ethiek en huisdieren, in: *Filosofie en Praktijk*, vol. 14 no. 4, winter 1993, p. 199-211.

Visser, M. B. H., en F. J. Grommers (red.), *Dier of ding; Objectivering van dieren*, Pudoc, Wageningen, 1988.

Visser, T., en H. Verhoog, De eigenwaarde van dieren en het dierenrecht, in: *Filosofie en Praktijk*, vol. 7 no. 3, sept. 1986, p. 113-132 (+ vol. 7 no. 4, dec. 1986, p. 198-208).

Anthropology, philosophical (incl. hermeneutics)

Cheetham, T., The Forms of Life: Complexity, History, and Actuality, in: *Environmental Ethics*, vol. 15 no. 4, Winter 1993, p. 293-312.

Coolen, T. M. T., Over de maat van het maken, in: B. Nagel (red.), *Maken en Breken; over productie en spiritualiteit*, Kok/Agora, Kampen, 1988, p. 67-93.

Coolen, T. M. T., Enkele filosofisch-anthropologische notities over het maken, in: W. Achterberg (red.) 1989, p. 46-65.

Coolen, T. M. T., Naar een hermeneutiek van de natuur; of: over de noodzaak distantie te verdragen, in: W. Zweers (red.) 1991, p. 112-119.

Coolen, T. M. T., *De machine voorbij; Over het zelfbegrip van de mens in het tijdperk van de informatietechniek*, Boom, Meppel, 1992.

Dewey, J., *Experience and Nature*, Dover, New-York, 1958 (1929).

Dryzek, J., Green Reason: Communicative Ethics for the Biosphere, in: *Environmental Ethics*, vol. 12 no. 3, Fall 1990, p. 195-211.

Gardiner, R. W., Between two worlds: Humans in nature and culture, in: *Environmental Ethics*, vol. 12 no. 4, Winter 1990, p. 339-353.

Kockelkoren, P., De muis in de klauwen van de kat. Een kader voor een hermeneutiek van de natuur, in: W. Zweers (red.) 1991, p. 97-112.

Kockelkoren, P., *De natuur van de goede verstaander*, Universiteit Twente, Enschede, Faculteit Wijsbegeerte en Maatschappijwetenschappen, wmw-publikatie no. 11, 1992.

Lemaire, T., *Over de waarde van culturen*, Ambo, Baarn, 1976.

Lemaire, T., *Binnenwegen; Essays en excursies*, Ambo, Baarn, 1988.

Midgley, M., *Beast and Man; The Roots of Human Nature*, Methuen, London, 1979.

Plessner, H., *Die Stufen des Organischen und der Mensch; Einleitung in die philosophische Anthropologie*, De Gruyter, Berlin, 1975 (1928)

Wal, G. A. van der, De maakbaarheid der dingen, in: W. Achterberg (red.) 1989, p. 23-46.

Attitudes towards nature (incl. paradigms)

(Anonymous), *Natuur tussen de oren; Natuur- en landschapsbeeldem en hun rol bij de ontwikkeling en vormgeving van beleid*, Natuurbeschermingsraad, Utrecht, 1993.

Achterberg, W., Milieuproblematiek en houdingen tegenover de natuur, in: M. Mentzel, (red.), *Milieubeleid normatief bezien*, Stenfert Kroese, Leiden, 1993, p. 43-65.

Amstel, A.R. van, e.a., *Vijf visies op natuurbehoud en natuurontwikkeling; Knelpunten en perspectieven van deze visies in het licht van de huidige maatschappelijke ontwikkelingen*, Raad voor Milieu- en Natuuronderzoek, Rijswijk, 1988.

Blom, P. J. B., *Grondhoudingen, natuurbeelden en natuurvisies in de Nederlandse natuurbescherming*, Vakgroep Natuurwetenschap en Samenleving, Univ. Utrecht, 1994.

Colby, M. E., *Ecology, Economics and Social Systems; The Evolution of the Relationship
between Environmental Management and Development*, UMI Diss. Serv,. Univ. of
Pennsylvania, 1990.

Kockelkoren, P., Grondhoudingen in de natuurbenadering: historisch en hedendaags, in:
P. Kockelkoren (red.), *Boven de groene zoden; Een filosofische benadering van milieu,
wetenschap en techniek*, Uitgeverij Jan van Arkel, Utrecht, 1990, p. 7-33.

Rodman, J., Paradigm Change in Political Science; An Ecological Perspective, in:
American Behavioral Scientist, vol. 24 no. 1, sept./oct. 1980 (spec. issue.: "Ecology and
the Social Sciences: An Emerging Paradigm"), p. 49-79.

Rodman, J., Four forms of ecological consciousness reconsidered, in: D. Scherer and T.
Attig (Eds.) 1983, p. 82-93.

Routley, R., Roles and Limits of Paradigms in Environmental Thought and Action, in:
R. Elliott and A. Gare (Eds.) 1983, p. 260-294.

Westhoff, V., De verantwoordelijkheid van de mens jegens de natuur (niet-westerse en
westerse houdingen), in: K. van Koppen e. a. (red.) 1984, p. 4-23.

Zweers, W., Houdingen ten opzichte van de natuur, in: *Heidemijtijdschrift*, vol. 100, 1989
no. 3, p. 74-80.

Zweers,W., Radicalisme of historisch besef? Over breuken en continuiteit in de grond-
houdingendiscussie, in: W. Zweers (red.) 1991, p. 63-71.

Biology

Augros R., en G. Stanciu, *De nieuwe biologie; doorbraak in de wetenschap van het leven*,
Rotterdam, 1989.

Bateson, G., *Steps to an Ecology of Mind*, Ballantine, New-York 1980 (1972).

Bateson, G., *Mind and nature; A necessary unity*, Fontana/Collins, London, 1980.

Bateson, G., and M. C. Bateson, *Angels Fear; Towards an Epistemology of the Sacred*,
Bantam Books, New-York, 1987.

Bateson, M. C., *Our Own Metaphor; A Personal Account of a Conference on the Effects of
Conscious Purpose on Human Adaptation*, Knopf, New-York, 1972.

Birch, C.,The Postmodern Challenge to Biology, in: Griffin, D. R. (Ed.), *The
Reenchantment of Science; Postmodern Proposals*, State University of New-York Press,
Albany, 1988, p. 69-79.

Birch, C., and J. B. Cobb Jr, *The liberation of life; From the cell to the community*,
Cambridge U. P., 1981.

Griffin, D. R., Of Minds and Molecules: Postmodern Medicine in a Psychosomatic
Universe, in: D. R. Griffin (Ed.) 1988 (see above), p. 141-165.

Keller, E. Fox, *A Feeling for the Organism: The Life and Work of Barbara MacClintock*,
Freeman, San Francisco, 1983 (also in Dutch).

Maas, M., *Gaia: machine of organisme; Op zoek naar een niet-mechanistische opvatting van
de Gaia- hypothese*, Uitgeverij Jan van Arkel, Utrecht, 1995.

Maas, T., De natuur als tautologie (een inleiding in het denken van Gregory Bateson), in:
W. Achterberg en W. Zweers (red.) 1986, p. 73-105.

Maturana, H. and F. Varela, *Autopoiësis and Cognition; The Realization of the Living*, Reidel, Dordrecht, 1980.

Monod, J., *Chance and Necessity: an Essay on the Natural Philosophy of Modern Biology*, New-York, Vintage Books, 1972.

Peacocke, A., *God and the New Biology*, Dent, London, 1986.

Sheldrake, R., *A New Science of Life; the Hypothesis of Formative Causation*, Granada, Blond and Briggs,London, 1981 (also in Dutch: *Een Nieuwe Levenswetenschap; De hypothese van de vormgevende oorzakelijkheid*, Mirananda, Wassenaar, 1983).

Sheldrake, R., The Laws of Nature as Habits: A Postmodern Basis for Science, in: D. R. Griffin (Ed.) 1988 (see above), p. 79-87.

Sheldrake, R., *The Presence of the Past; Morphic Resonance and the Habits of Nature*, Collins, London, 1988.

Sheldrake, R., *The Rebirth of Nature; The Greening of Science and of God*, Century, London, 1990.

Soontiëns, F., Biologie en anthropomorfisme, in: *Wijsgerig Perspectief op Maatschappij en Wetenschap*, vol. 31, 1990-91 no. 3, p. 76-81.

Soontiëns, F. J. K., *Natuurfilosofie en milieu-ethiek; Een teleologische natuurfilosofie als voorwaarde voor een milieu-ethiek*, Boom, Meppel, 1993.

Deep Ecology

Attfield, R., Sylvan, Fox and Deep Ecology: A View from the Continental Shelf, in: *Environmental Values*, vol. 2 no. 1, Spring 1993, p. 21-33.

Curtin, D., Dogen, Deep Ecology, and the Ecological Self, in: *Environmental Ethics*, vol. 16 no. 2, Summer 1994, p. 195-215.

Devall, B., The Deep Ecology Movement, in: *Natural Resources Journal*, vol. 20, Spring 1980, p. 299-323.

Devall B., and G. Sessions, *Deep Ecology, living as if nature mattered*, Peregrine Smith Books, Salt Lake City, 1985.

Fox, W., Deep Ecology: a New Philosophy of our Time?, in: *The Ecologist*, vol. 14, 1984 no. 5-6, p. 194-205.

Fox, W., Approaching Deep Ecology: A Response to Richard Sylvan's Critique of Deep Ecology, *Environmental Studies Occasional Paper* 20, Univ. of Tasmania, Hobart, 1986.

Fox, W., On the Interpretation of Naess" Central Term "Self-realization", in: *The Trumpeter*, vol. 7 no. 2, Spring 1990, p. 98-101.

Fox, W., *Toward a Transpersonal Ecology; Developing New Foundations for Environmentalism*, Shambala, Boston, 1990.

Naess, A., The Shallow and the Deep, Long-Range Movement, a Summary, in: *Inquiry*, vol. 16, 1973, p. 95-100.

Naess, A., Self-realization: an Ecological Approach to Being in the World, in: J. Seed a. o., 1988 (see below), p. 19-32 (orig. in: *The Trumpeter*, vol. 4 no. 3, Summer 1987, p. 35-42).

Naess, A., Intuition, Intrinsic Value, and Deep Ecology, in: *The Ecologist*, vol. 14, 1984 no. 5-6, p. 201-203.

Naess, A., Deep Ecology and Ultimate Premises, in: *The Ecologist*, vol. 18, 1988 no. 4-5, p. 128-132.

Naess, A., *Ecology, Community and Lifestyle* (ed. by D. Rothenberg), Cambridge University Press, Cambridge, 1989.

Naess, A., "Man apart" and Deep Ecology: a reply to Reed, in: *Environmental Ethics*, vol. 12 no. 2, Summer 1990, p. 185-193 (see also Reed).

Naess, A., The encouraging richness and diversity of ultimate premises in environmental philosophy, in: *The Trumpeter*, vol. 9 no. 2, Spring 1992, p. 53-61 (whole issue on Naess).

Naess, A., Beautiful Action. Its Function in the Ecological Crisis, in: *Environmental Values*, vol. 2 no. 1, Spring 1993, p. 67-71.

Naess, A., *Spinoza and the Deep Ecology Movement*, Eburon, Delft, Meded. Spinozahuis no. 67, 1993.

Reed, P., Man Apart: an Alternative to the Self-realization Approach, in: *Environmental Ethics*, vol. 11 no. 1, Spring 1989, p. 53-71 (see also Naess 1990).

Seed, J., Anthropocentrism, Appendix E, in: B. Devall and G. Sessions 1985 (see above), p. 243-247.

Seed, J., J. Macy, P. Fleming and A. Naess, *Thinking Like a Mountain; Towards a Council of All Beings*, New Society Publishers, Philadelphia, 1988.

Sessions, G., Shallow and Deep Ecology: a Review of the Philosophical Literature, in: R. C. Schultz and J. D. Hughes (Eds.) 1981, p. 391-463.

Sessions, G., Arne Naess and the Union of Theory and Practice, in: *The Trumpeter*, vol. 9 no. 2, Spring 1992, p. 73-77.

Sessions, G. (Ed.), *Deep Ecology in the 21th. century*, Shambala, Boston, 1994.

Sylvan, R., A Critique of Deep Ecology, in: *Radical Ecology*, 1985, no. 40, p. 2-12, and no. 41, p. 10-22.

Zweers, W., Deep Ecology, in: *Wijsgerig Perspectief op Maatschappij en Wetenschap*, vol. 34 no. 6, 1993/94, p. 174-180.

Developing countries

(Anonymous), *Economy, Ecology and Spirituality; Toward a Theory and Practice of Sustainability*, The Asian NGO Coalition (Manila), IRED Asia (Colombo), The People-Centered Development Forum (New-York), Aug. 1993.

Charkiewicz-Pluta, E., and S. Häusler (with R. Braidotti and S. Wieringa), *Remaking the World Together; Women, the Environment and Sustainable Development*, Institute of Social Studies/Department of Women's Studies University of Utrecht, 1991.

Court, T. de la, *Beyond Brundtland; Green Development in the 1990s*, Zed Books, London, 1990.

Court, T. de la, *Different Worlds; Environment and development beyond the nineties*, Uitgeverij Jan van Arkel, Utrecht, 1992.

Curtin, D., Making Peace with the Earth: Indigenous Agriculture and the Green Revolution, in: *Environmental Ethics*, vol. 17 no. 1, Spring 1995, p. 59-74.

Engel, J. R., and J. G., (Eds.), *Ethics of Environment and Development; Global Challenge and International Response*, Belhaven Press, London, 1990.

Guha, R., Radical American Environmentalism and Wilderness Preservation: a Third World Critique, in: *Environmental Ethics*, vol. 11 no. 1, Spring 1989, p. 71-85 (see also Johns).

Hombergh, H. van den, *Gender, Environment and Development; A guide to the literature*, Uitgeverij Jan van Arkel, Utrecht, 1993.

Johns, D. M., The Relevance of Deep Ecology to the Third World, in: *Environmental Ethics*, vol. 12 no. 3, Fall 1990, p. 233-253 (reply to Guha).

Luijff, R., and P. Tijmes, Kanttekeningen bij het Brundtlandrapport, in: P. Kockelkoren (Ed.), *Boven de groene zoden; Een filosofische benadering van milieu, wetenschap en techniek*, Uitgeverij Jan van Arkel, Utrecht, 1990, p. 59-71.

Sachs, W., Environment and Development: the Story of a Dangerous Liaison, in: *The Ecologist*, vol. 21 no. 6, nov./dec. 1991, p. 252-258.

Sachs, W., (Ed.), *Global Ecology; A New Arena of Political Conflict*, Zed Books, London, 1993.

Schrijvers, J., *The Violence of Development; A Choice for Intellectuals* (*De boodschap van het vijfde ontwikkelingsdecennium*), Uitgeverij Jan van Arkel/Institute of Development Research Amsterdam, Utrecht/Amsterdam, 1992.

Schrijvers, J., Participation and Power; a Transformative Research Perspective, in: N. Nelson and S. Wright (Eds.), *Power and Participatory Research. Theory and Practice*, Intermediate Technology Publications, Rugby, 1994 (in press).

Shiva, V., *Staying alive: women, ecology and development*, Zed Books, London, 1989.

Terhal, P., Milieu en ontwikkeling, in: G. A. van der Wal en R. M. Hogendoorn (red.) 1993, p. 33-43.

Ecofeminism

Cheney, J., Ecofeminism and Deep Ecology, in: *Enviromental Ethics*, vol. 11 no. 4, Summer 1987, p. 115-145.

Diamond, I., and G. F. Orenstein (Eds.), *Reweaving the World; The Emergence of Ecofeminism*, Sierra Club Books, San Francisco, 1990.

Fox, W., The Deep Ecology-Ecofeminism Debate and its Parallels, in: *Environmental Ethics*, vol. 11 no. 1, Spring 1989, p. 5-27.

Green, K., Freud, Wollstonecraft, and Ecofeminism: A Defense of Liberal Feminism, in: *Environmental Ethics*, vol. 16 no. 2, Summer 1994, p. 117-135.

Griffin, S., *Women and Nature*, Harper and Row, New-York, 1978.

Groen, E. de, De vrouw als reddende engel van het milieu; Draaft het ecofeminisme niet een beetje door?, in: *Opzij*, mei 1992, p. 88-92.

Grond, A., De relatie tussen feminisme en milieufilosofie, in: W. van Dooren en T. Hoff (red.), *Aktueel filosoferen; Nederlands-Vlaamse filosofiedag Delft 1993*, Eburon, Delft, 1993, p. 295-301.

Keller, E. Fox, *Reflections on Gender and Science*, Yale Univ. Press, New Haven/London, 1985 (also in Dutch).

Matthews, F., Relating to nature: Deep Ecology or Ecofeminism?, in: *The Trumpeter*, vol. 11 no. 4, Fall 1994, p. 159-167.

Petit-Grond, A., *De Mythe van de Zeemeermin; een feministische bijdrage aan het milieude-bat*, Universiteit van Amsterdam, Faculteit Wijsbegeerte, 1993.

Plant, J., (Ed.), *Healing the Wounds; The Promise of Ecofeminism*, New Society Publishers, Philadelphia, 1989.

Plumwood, V., Nature, Self, and Gender: Feminism, Environmental Philosophy, and the Critique of Rationalism, in: *Hypatia*, vol. 6, 1991.

Plumwood, V., Feminism and Ecofeminism; Beyond the Dualistic Assumptions of Women, Men and Nature, in: *The Ecologist*, vol. 22 no. 1, jan/feb. 1992, p. 8-14.

Plumwood, V., *Feminism and the Mastery of Nature*, Routledge, London, 1993.

Salleh, A. K., Deeper than Deep Ecology: the Eco-Feminist Connection, in: *Environmental Ethics*, vol. 6 no. 4, Winter 1984, p. 339-347.

Salleh, A. K., The Ecofeminism/Deep Ecology Debate, in: *Environmental Ethics*, vol. 14 no. 3, Fall 1992, p. 195-217.

Simmons, P., Editorial: The Challenge of Feminism, in: *The Ecologist*, vol. 22 no. 1, jan./feb. 1992, p. 2-4.

Warren, K., Feminism and Ecology: Making Connections, in: *Environmental Ethics*, vol. 9 no. 1, Spring 1987, p. 3-21.

Warren, K., The Power and Promise of Ecological Feminism, in: *Environmental Ethics*, vol. 12 no. 2, Summer 1990, p. 125-147.

Warren K. (Ed.), *Ecological Feminism*, Routledge, London, 1994.

Zimmerman, M., Feminism, Deep Ecology and Environmental Ethic, in: *Environmental Ethics*, vol. 9 no. 1, Spring 1987, p. 21-45.

Ecological world view (incl. "Gaia")

(Anonymous), Rethinking Man and Nature: Towards an Ecological Worldview, spec. issue of *The Ecologist*, 1988, vol. 18 no. 4-5.

Bunyard, P., and E. Goldsmith (Eds.), *Gaia: the Thesis, the Mechanisms and the Implications; Proceedings of the First Annual Camelford Conference on the Implications of the Gaia Thesis*, Wadebridge Ecological Center, 1988.

Bunyard, P., and E. Goldsmith (Eds.), *Gaia and Evolution; Proceedings of the Second Annual Camelford Conference on the Implications of the Gaia Thesis*, Wadebridge Ecological Center, 1989.

Callicott, J. Baird, The Metaphysical Implications of Ecology, in: *Environmental Ethics*, vol. 8 no. 4, Winter 1986, p. 301-317 (also in: J. B. Callicott 1989, p. 101-117).

Coolen, T. M. T., en R. Kleiss, Ecologie en ideologie, in: *Algemeen Nederlands Tijdschrift voor Wijsbegeerte*, vol. 73 no. 1, febr. 1981, p. 20-44.

Drengson, A., *Shifting Paradigms; From Technocrat to Planetary Person*, Lightstar Press, Victoria, 1983.

Goldsmith, E, *The Way: An Ecological World-View*, in: *The Ecologist*, vol. 18, 1988 no. 4/5, p. 160-186.

Goldsmith, E., Toward a biospheric ethic, in: *The Ecologist*, vol. 19, 1989 no. 2, p. 68-76.

Goldsmith, E., Gaia and Evolution, in: *The Ecologist*, vol. 19, 1989 no. 4, p. 147-154.

Goldsmith, E., The Way: An Ecological Worldview, Shambala, Boston, 1993 (oorspr. Rider, London, 1992).

Lemaire, T., Een nieuwe aarde (utopie en ecologie), in: W. Achterberg en W. Zweers (red.) 1986, p. 257-289.

Leopold, A., *A sand county almanac and sketches here and there*, Oxford University Press, London, 1980 (1949).

Lovelock, J. E., *Gaia: a new look at life on earth*, Oxford University Press, Oxford, 1979.

Lovelock, J. E., *The Ages of Gaia*, Oxford University Press, Oxford, 1989.

Maas, M., *Gaia, machine of organisme; een onderzoek naar een mogelijke niet-mechanistische opvatting van de Gaia-hypothese*, Uitgeverij Jan van Arkel, Utrecht, 1995.

Mathews, F., *The Ecological Self*, Routledge, London, 1991.

Oehlschlaeger, M., (Ed.), *The Wilderness Condition; Essays on Environment and Civilization*, Island Press, Washington, 1992.

Roszak Th., *Where the Wasteland Ends*, 1972 (*Het einde van niemandsland; Politiek en transcendentie in de post-industriële samenleving*, Meulenhoff, Amsterdam, 1974).

Roszak, Th., The Sacramental Vision of Nature, in: R. Clarke (Ed.), *Notes for the Future*, Thames and Hudson, London, 1975, p. 107-115.

Roszak, Th., *The Voice of the Earth*, Simon and Schuster, New-York, 1992.

Skolimowski, H., *Eco-Philosophy; Designing New tactics for Living*, Boyars, London, 1981.

Skolimowski, H., Eco-philosophy and Deep Ecology, in: *The Ecologist*, vol. 18, 1988 no. 4-5, p. 124-128.

Tobias, M., (Ed.), *Deep Ecology*, Avant Books, San Diego, 1985.

Turner, F., *Rebirth of Value; Meditations on Beauty, Ecology, Religion, and Education*, State University of New-York Press, Albany, 1991.

Weston, A., Forms of Gaian Ethics, in: *Environmental Ethics*, vol. 9 no. 3, Fall 1987, p. 217-231.

Zoeteman, K., *Gaiasofie; Anders kijken naar evolutie, ruimtelijke ordening en milieubeheer*, Ankh-Hermes, Deventer, 1989.

Zweers, W., Natuur en cultuur in ecologisch perspectief, in: W. Achterberg en W. Zweers (red.) 1984, p. 97-142.

Zweers, W., *Participeren aan de natuur; Ontwerp voor een ecologisering van het wereldbeeld*, Uitgeverij Jan van Arkel, Utrecht, 1995.

Ecological and Environmental Science

Boersema, J. J., De kwaliteit van het milieu en de kwaliteit van ons bestaan, in: *Filosofie en Praktijk*, vol. 14 no. 2, zomer 1993, p. 57-69.

Commoner, B., *The Closing Circle; Confronting the Environmental Crisis*, Cape, London, 1972.

Daele, W. van den, en J. Cramer, Ecologie: een "alternatieve" natuurwetenschap?, in: *Kennis en Methode*, vol. 7, 1983 no. 2, p. 121-137.

Groot, W. de, Waarden in analyse, waarden in actie en waarden in de maak: normativiteit in milieukunde en ecologie, in: W. Achterberg en W. Zweers (red.) 1986, p. 135-175.

Groot, W. T. de, *Natuurgerichte normstelling*, Mededelingen Raad voor Milieu- en Natuuronderzoek, Rijswijk, 1989.

Groot, W. T. de, *Environmental Science Theory; Concepts and Methods in a One-World, Problem-Oriented Paradigm*, Elsevier, Amsterdam, 1992.

Kormondy, E. J., Human intervention into natural ecosystems: the scientific background to moral choice, in: R. Schultz and J. Hughes (Eds.) 1981, p. 23-43.

Quispel, A., De plaats van de mens in de biosfeer, in: K. van Koppen e. a. (red.) 1984, p. 70-81.

Schroevers, P. J., Ecosystemen, hun opbouw en afbraak, een theoretisch model, in: *Ekologie*, 1980 no. 1, p. 4-13.

Schroevers, P. J., De natuur als een randvoorwaarde, in: K. v. Koppen e. a. (red.) 1984, p. 91-107.

Schroevers, P. J., Inhoud en betekenis van een holistisch natuurbeeld, in: W. Achterberg en W. Zweers (red.) 1984, p. 49-74.

Schroevers, P. J, Veranderend natuurbegrip in de ecologie, in: *Filosofie en Praktijk*, vol. 11 no. 1, maart 1990, p. 28-45

Schroevers, P. J., Natuurbeleid en natuurbegrip, in: *Filosofie en Praktijk*, vol. 14 no. 2, zomer 1993, p. 91-103.

Schroevers, P. J. (red.), *Landschapstaal; een stelsel van basisbegrippen voor de landschapsecologie*, Pudoc, Wageningen, 1982.

Sloet van Oldruitenborgh, C. J. M., Natuur en mens vanuit ecologie en natuurbeheer, in: K. van Koppen e. a. (red.) 1984, p. 81-91.

Verhoog, H., Ekologie als "alternatieve" wetenschap, in: W. Achterberg en W. Zweers (red.) 1984, p. 74-97.

History

Attfield, R., Western Traditions and Environmental Ethics, in: R. Elliot and A. Gare (Eds.) 1983, p. 201-231.

Berman, M., *The Reenchantment of the World*, Cornell University Press, Ithaca, 1981.

Berman, M., *Coming to Our Senses; Body and Spirit in the Hidden History of the West*, Simon and Schuster, New-York, 1989.

Boersema, J. J., "Eerst de Jood maar ook de Griek"; op zoek naar de wortels van het milieuprobleem in de westerse cultuur, in: W. Zweers (red.) 1991, p. 27-57.

Braeckman, A., Schellings natuurfilosofie en moderniteitskritiek, in: *Wijsgerig Perspectief op Maatschappij en Wetenschap*, vol. 31, 1990/91 no. 1, p. 10-19.

Dessaur, C. I., *De droom der rede; Het mensbeeld in de sociale wetenschappen*, Nijhoff, Den Haag, 1982.

Dijksterhuis, E. J., *De mechanisering van het wereldbeeld; De geschiedenis van het natuurwetenschap pelijk denken*, Meulenhoff, Amsterdam, 1989 (1950).

Engelhardt, D. von, Spiritualisierung der Natur und Naturalisierung des Menschen. Perspektiven der romantische Naturforschung, in: F. Rapp (Hrsg.), *Naturverständnis und Naturbeherrschung*, Fink, München, 1981, p. 96-111.

Glacken, C. J., *Traces on the Rhodian Shore; Nature and Culture in Western Thought from Ancient Times to the End of the Eighteenth Century*, Univ. of California Press, Berkeley, 1990 (1967).

Hughes, D., *Ecology in Ancient Civilizations*, Univ. of New Mexico Press, 1975.

Lindberg, D. C., *The Beginnings of Western Science; The European Scientific Tradition in Philosophical, religious and Institutional Context*, 600 B. C. to A. D. 1450, Univ. of Chicago Press, 1992 (*Pioniers van de westerse wetenschap*, Boom, Meppel, 1994).

Marshall, P., *Nature's Web; Rethinking our Place on Earth*, Paragon House, New-York, 1994.

Mayer-Tasch, P. C. (Hrsg.), *Natur denken; Eine Genealogie der ökologischen Idee*, 2 vols., Fischer, Frankfurt am Main, 1991.

Merchant, C., *The Death of Nature; women, ecology and the scientific revolution*, Harper and Row, San Francisco, 1980.

Nash, R. F., *Wilderness and the American Mind*, Yale Univ. Press, 1982 (1967).

Nash, R. F., *The Rights of nature; A History of Environmental Ethics*, Univ. of Wisconsin Press, Madison, 1989.

Oehlschlaeger, M., *The Idea of Wilderness, From Prehistory to the Age of ecology*, Yale Univ. Press, New Haven, 1991.

Ponting, C., *A Green History of the World*, Penguin Books, Harmondsworth, 1992 (also in Dutch).

Tijmes, P., Afscheid van het anthropocentrisme? in: *Wijsgerig Perspectief op Maatschappij en Wetenschap*, vol. 34 no. 6, 1993/94, p. 180-187.

Verhoog, Milieu-ethiek en de natuurfilosofie van Goethe, in: K. van Koppen e. a. (red.) 1984, p. 32-44.

Verhoog, H., Lezen in het boek der natuur, in: W. Achterberg (red.) 1989, p. 141-159.

Verhoog, Lezen in het boek der natuur: vroeger en nu, in: G. A. van der Wal en R. M. Hogendoorn (red.) 1993, p. 1-11.

Wall, D., *Green History; a reader in environmental literature, philosophy and politics*, Routledge, London, 1994.

White, L., The Historical Roots of our Ecologic Crisis, in: *Science*, 155, 1967, no. 37, p. 1203-1207 (also in: I. G. Barbour (Ed.) 1973).

White, L., Continuing the Conversation, in: I. G. Barbour (Ed.) 1973, p. 55-66.

Worster, D., *Nature's Economy: A History of Ecological Ideas*, Cambridge Univ. Press, Cambridge, 1977.

Intrinsic value

Achterberg, W., De intrinsieke waarde van de natuur, in: *Filosofie en Praktijk*, vol. 10 no. 2, juni 1989, p. 67-86.

Callicott, J. Baird, Intrinsic Value, Quantum Theory, and Environmental Ethics, in: *Environmenal Ethics*, vol. 7 no. 3, Fall1985, p. 257-277 (also in: J. B. Callicott 1989, p. 157-177).

Callicott, J. Baird, On the Intrinsic Value of Nonhuman Species, in: J. B. Callicott 1989, p. 129-157.

Callicott, J. Baird, Rolston on Intrinsic Value: a Deconstruction, in: *Environmental Ethics*, vol. 14 no. 2, Summer 1992, p. 129-145.

Kasanmoentalib, S., De intrinsieke waarde van de natuur, in: *Filosofie en Praktijk*, vol. 15 no. 3, najaar 1994, p. 130-143.

Meijers, A. W. M. en M. S. van der Schaar, Realistische of antirealistische milieufilosofie? In discussie met: W. Achterberg en W. Zweers (red.), Milieucrisis en Filosofie, in: *Algemeen Nederlands Tijdschrift voor Wijsbegeerte*, vol. 78 no. 4, okt. 1986, p. 251-262.

Musschenga, A. W., Anthropocentrisme en de intrinsieke waarde van de niet-menselijke natuur, in: *Filosofie en Praktijk*, vol. 15 no. 3, najaar 1994, p. 113-130.

Rolston, H., Values in Nature, in: *Environmental Ethics*, vol. 3 no. 2, Summer 1981, p. 113-129 (also in: H. Rolston 1986, p. 74-91).

Rolston, H., Are values in nature subjective or objective?, in: *Environmental Ethics*, vol. 4 no. 2, Summer 1982, p. 125-153 (also in: H. Rolston 1986, p. 91-118).

Zimmerman, M., Quantum Theory, Intrinsic Value and Pantheïsm, in: *Environmental Ethics*, vol. 10 no. 1, Spring 1988, p. 3-31.

Zweers, W., Intrinsieke waarde van de natuur, in: *Algemeen Nederlands Tijdschrift voor Wijsbegeerte*, vol. 79 no. 2, april 1987, p. 137-144.

Zweers, W., Intrinsieke waarde als begrenzing van het maken, in: W. Achterberg (red.) 1989, p. 65-85.

Marxism

Enzensberger, H. M. (Hrsg.), *Ökologie und Politik, oder Die Zukunft der Industrialisierung*, Kursbuch no. 33, oct. 1973.

Gorz, A., *Ecologie en vrijheid; Politieke opstellen over milieu, energie en economische groei*, Van Gennep, Amsterdam, 1978.

Harmsen, G., *Natuur, geschiedenis, filosofie*, Oratie Groningen, SUN, Nijmegen, 1974.

Lee, D. C., On the Marxian view of the relationship between man and nature, in: *Environmental Ethics*, vol. 2 no. 1, Spring 1980, p. 3-16.

Lee, D. C., Toward a Marxian ecological ethic: a response to two critics, in: *Environmental Ethics*, vol. 4 no. 4, Winter 1982, p. 339-345.

Leiss, W., *The Domination of Nature*, Braziller, New-York, 1972.

Mehte, W., *Oekologie und Marxismus; Ein Neuansatz zur Rekonstruktion der politischen Oekonomie unter ökologischen Krisenbedingungen*, SOAK Verlag, Hannover, 1983 (1981).

Parsons, H. L., *Marx and Engels on Ecology*, Greenwood Press, Westport, 1977.

Routledge, V., On Karl Marx as an environmental hero, in: *Environmental Ethics*, vol. 3 no. 3, Fall 1981, p. 237-245.

Schmidt, A., *Der Begriff der Natur in der Lehre von Marx*, Europäische Verlagsanstalt, Frankfurt am Main, 1978 (1962).

Tolman, C., Karl Marx, alienation and the mastery of nature, in: *Environmental Ethics*, vol. 3 no. 1, Spring 1981, p. 63-74.

Verhagen H. (red.), *Inleiding tot de politieke economie van het milieu*, Ekologische Uitgeverij, Amsterdam, 1978.

Non-western cultures

(Anonymous), *Het verhaal Aarde; Inheemse volken aan het woord over milieu en ontwikkeling*, Novib, Den Haag, 1992.

(Anonymous), *Hoe kun je de lucht bezitten; Een indiaanse visie op het beheer van de aarde*, Aktie Strohalm /Ekologische Uitgeverij, Utrecht, 1980.

(Anonymous), *Wij zijn een deel van de aarde: teksten van Indianen*, (foto's Edward Curtis, voorwoord Ton Lemaire), Uitgeverij Jan van Arkel, Utrecht, 1988.

Ames, R. T., Taoism and the Nature of Nature, in: *Environmental Ethics*, vol. 8 no. 4, Winter 1986, p. 317-351.

Breeveld, J., *De risico's van het denken: Het treffen tussen Indiaanse spiritualiteit en techniek*, Uitgeverij Jan van Arkel, Utrecht, 1992.

Callicott, J. Baird, Traditional American Indian and Western European Attitudes toward Nature: an Overview, in: *Environmental Ethics*, vol. 4 no. 4, Winter 1982, p. 293-319 (also in: J. B. Callicott 1989, p. 177-203).

Callicott, J. Baird, *Earth's Insight: A Multicultural Survey of Ecological Ethics from the Mediterranean Basin to the Australian Outback*, Univ. of California Press, Berkeley, 1994.

Callicott, J. Baird, and R. T. Ames (Eds.), *Nature in Asian Traditions of Thought*, State Univ. of New-York Press, 1989.

Deutsch, E., A Metaphysical Grounding for Nature Reverence: East-West, in: *Environmental Ethics*, vol. 8 no. 4, Winter 1986, p. 293-301.

Elders, F., Humanisme tussen Oost en West; Over boeddhisme, christendom en humanisme, in: P. B. Cliteur en D.J. van Houten (red.), *Humanisme; Theorie en Praktijk*, De Tijdstroom, Utrecht, 1993, p. 81-99.

Lemaire, T., De Indiaanse houding tegenover de natuur, in: W. Achterberg en W. Zweers (red.) 1984, p. 171-189.

Lemaire. T., *De Indiaan in ons bewustzijn; De ontmoeting van de Oude met de Nieuwe Wereld*, Ambo, Baarn, 1986.

Moody, P., (Ed.), *The Indigenous Voice; Visions and Realities*, International Books, Utrecht, 1993 (1988).

Norberg-Hodge, H., *Ancient Futures; Learning from Ladakh*, Sierra Club Books, San Francisco, 1991.

Westhoff, V., Het natuurbeeld in schriftloze culturen en in hoger ontwikkelde oosterse wereldbeschouwingen, in: W. Achterberg (red.) 1989, p. 177-199.

Physics (incl. Science, general)

(Anonymous), David Bohm's Implicate Order: Physics, Philosophy, and Theology, spec. issue of *Zygon, Journal of Religion and Science*, vol. 20 no. 2, June 1985.

Bohm, D., The implicate or enfolded order: a new order for physics, in: J. Cobb and D. R. Griffin (Eds.), *Mind in Nature; essays on the interface of science and philosophy*, University Press of America, Washinton, 1977.

Bohm, D., *Wholeness and the Implicate Order*, Routledge, London, 1981.

Bohm, D., Postmodern Science and a Postmodern World, in: D. R. Griffin (Ed.) 1988 (see below), p. 57-69.

Bohm, D., and F. D. Peat, *Science, Order, and Creativity*, Bantam Books, New-York, 1987.

Burtt, E. A., *The Metaphysical Foundations of Modern Physical Science*, Routledge, London, 1980 (1924).

Capra, F., *The Tao of Physics*, Wildwood House, London, 1975.

Capra, F., *The Turning Point; Science, Society and the Rising Culture*, Wildwood House, London, 1982.

Davies, P., *God and the New Physics*, Dent, London, 1983.

Derkse, W. (red.), *Het heil van de natuurwetenschap?*, Uitgverij Gooi en Sticht, Baarn, 1993.

Erkelens, H. van, *Einstein, Jung en de relativiteit van God*, Kok/Agora, Kampen, 1988.

Factor, D. (Ed.), *Unfolding Meaning: a week-end of dialogue with David Bohm*, Foundation House Publishers, Mickleton, 1985.

Griffin, D. R. (Ed.), *The Reenchantment of Science; Postmodern Proposals*, State University of New-York Press, Albany, 1988 (Introduction: The Reenchantment of Science, by D. R. Griffin, p. 1-47).

Jantsch, E., *The Self-Organizing Universe; Scientific and Human Implications of the Emerging Paradigm of Evolution*, Pergamon Press, Oxford, 1980.

Kayzer, W. (red.), *Een schitterend ongeluk*, Contact, Amsterdam, 1993.

Prigogine, I., and I. Stengers, *Order out of chaos; man's new dialogue with nature*, Heinemann, London, 1984 (*Orde uit Chaos*, Bert Bakker, Amsterdam, 1985).

Rietdijk, C. W., De moderne fysica: suggestie van een verborgen werkelijkheid, in: *Civis Mundi*, vol. 26, juni 1987, p. 74-81.

Rietdijk, C. W., *Experimenten met God*, BRT, Brussel, 1989.

Tennekes, H., De ecologisering van een meteoroloog, in: W. Zweers (red.) 1991, p. 73-87 (comments by C. Kwa and P. Schroevers).

Wilber, K. (Ed.), *The holographic paradigm and other paradoxes: exploring the leading edge of science*, Shambala, Boulder, 1982 (a. o. contrib. on holography, physics/mysticism, New Age, and conversations with Bohm, Capra and Wilber).

Policy, Politics, Democracy

(Anonymous), *Caring for the Earth; a Strategy for Sustainable Living*, IUCN/UNEP/WWF, Gland, 1993.

(Anonymous), *Duurzame risico's: een blijvend gegeven*, Wetenschappelijke Raad voor het regeringsbeleid, Staatsuitgeverij, Den Haag, 1994.

(Anonymous), *Het Milieu: denkbeelden voor de 21e eeuw*, Commissie Lange Termijn Milieubeleid, Kerckebosch, Zeist, 1990.

(Anonymous), *Nationaal Milieubeleidsplan*, Staatsuitgeverij, Den Haag, 1989.

(Anonymous), *Nationale Milieuverkenning* 1993-2015, RIVM, Samson, Alphen aan de Rijn, 1993.

(Anonymous), *Natuurbeleidsplan*, Staatsuitgeverij, Den Haag, 1989.

(Anonymous), *Our Common Future*, Oxford Univ. Press, Oxford, 1987 (The "Brundtland-report").

(Anonymous), *The Environment: Towards a Sustainable Future*, Dutch Committee for Long-Term Environmental Policy, Kluwer, Dordrecht, 1994.

(Anonymous), *Zorgen voor morgen; Nationale milieuverkenning* 1985-2010, RIVM, Bilthoven, 1988.

Achterberg, W., Kan de liberale democratie de milieucrisis overleven? Duurzame ontwikkeling tussen neutraliteit en perfectionisme, in: W. Zweers (red.) 1991, p. 129-156 (with comments by F. Jacobs and A. Musschenga).

Asperen, T. van, Milieu en overheid, in: W. Achterberg en W. Zweers (red.) 1986, p. 175-201.

Burg, W. van der, Het milieu in de politieke filosofie, in: W. Achterberg (red.) 1989, p. 96-121.

Capra, F., and C. Spretnak, *Green Politics; The Global Promise*, Hutchinson, London, 1984.

Dobson, A., *Green Political Theory*, Routledge, London, 1992.

Dobson, A., and P. Lucardie (Eds.), *The Politics of Nature; Explorations in Green Political Theory*, Routledge, London, 1993.

Dubbink, W., Democratie-theorie en de milieuproblematiek, in: *Filosofie en Praktijk*, vol. 15 no. 3, najaar 1994, p. 143-165.

Eckersley, R., *Environmentalism and Political Theory; Toward an Ecocentric Approach*, University College, London, 1992.

Geus, M. de, *Politiek, milieu en vrijheid*, Uitgeverij Jan van Arkel, Utrecht, 1993.

Huisman, H., Visies op het milieubeleid, in: K. van Koppen e. a. (red.) 1984, p. 108-119.

Kockelkoren P., De kloof tussen natuur en cultuur in het beleid, in: P. Kockelkoren (red.), *Boven de groene zoden; Een filosofische benadering van milieu, wetenschap en techniek*, Uitgeverij Jan van Arkel, Utrecht, 1990, p. 71-93.

Kockelkoren, P., W. Achterberg, H. Achterhuis and G. A. van der Wal, Environmental Policy in transformation: a philosophical approach, in: (Anonymous), *The Environment* (see above) 1994, p. 253-273.

Korthals, M., *Duurzaamheid en democratie; Sociaal-filosofische beschouwingen over milieubeleid, wetenschap en democratie*, Boom, Meppel, 1994.

Mentzel, M. A., and P. B. Lehning, A political basis for a sustainable society, in: (Anonymous), *The Environment* (see above) 1994, p. 443-463.

Mentzel, M., (red.), *Milieubeleid normatief bezien*, Stenfert Kroese, Leiden, 1993.

Nelissen, N., Milieubeleid: Experimenteren met nieuwe vormen van besturing?, in: G. A. van der Wal en R. M. Hogendoorn (red.) 1993, p. 49-59.

Steenbergen, B. van, Towards a Global Ecological Citizen, in: B. van Steenbergen (Ed.), *The Condition of Citizenship*, Sage, London, 1994, p. 141-153.

Tellegen, E., Milieu en staat; essay over een haat-liefde verhouding, in: W. Achterberg en W. Zweers (red.) 1984, p. 33-49.

Social and economic philosophy

Achterhuis, H., Het milieu als "commons", in: W. Achterberg en W. Zweers (red.) 1986, p. 201-231.

Achterhuis, H., *Het rijk van de schaarste; Van Thomas Hobbes tot Michel Foucault*, Ambo, Baarn, 1988.

Achterhuis, H., Natuur: begeerte en schaarste, in: W. Achterberg (red.) 1989, p. 121-141.

Achterhuis, H., Sociale ethiek of milieu-ethiek?, in: G. A. van der Wal en R. M. Hogendoorn (red.) 1993, p. 59-65.

Biesboer, F., (red.), *Greep op groei; Het thema van de jaren negentig*, Uitgeverij Jan van Arkel, Utrecht, 1993.

Bookchin, M., *The Ecology of Freedom; the Emergence and Dissolution of Hierarchy*, Cheshire Books, Palo Alto, 1982.

Bookchin, M., What is Social Ecology?, in: M. Zimmermann a. o. (Eds.) 1993, p. 354-373.

Eckersley, R., Divining Evolution: the Ecological Ethics of Murray Bookchin, in: *Environmental Ethics*, Vol. 11 no. 2, Summer 1989, p. 99-117.

Hardin, G., The tragedy of the commons, in: *Science*, vol. 162, 1968, p. 1243-1248.

Hueting, R., Hypocrisie, het voornaamste struikelblok voor milieubehoud, in: G. A. van der Wal en R. M. Hogendoorn (red.) 1993, p. 11-19.

Keulartz, J., *Strijd om de natuur; Kritiek van de sociale ecologie*, Boom, Meppel, 1995 (in press).

Opschoor, H., *Na ons geen zondvloed; Voorwaarden voor duurzaam milieugebruik*, Kok/Agora, Kampen, 1989.

Opschoor, J. B., Marktmechanische milieudegradatie, in: W. Zweers (red.) 1991, p. 173-192 (comments by H. Achterhuis and J. van der Straaten).

Pepper, D., *Eco-socialism; From Deep Ecology to Social Justice*, Routledge, London, 1993.

Schumacher, E. F., *Small is beautiful*, Blond and Briggs, London, 1973 (*Hou het klein: een economische studie waarbij de mens weer meetelt*, Ambo, Baarn).

Tawney, R., *The Acquisitive Society*, London, Bell, 1922.

Spirituality, Ecological experience

(Anonymous), Betekenis van spiritualiteit en spirituele bewegingen in onze tijd, spec. issue of *Civis Mundi*, vol. 24 no. 4, oct. 1986.

(Anonymous), Milieucrisis en spiritualiteit, spec. issue of *Speling; Tijdschrift voor bezinning*, vol. 46 no. 4, dec. 1994.

(Anonymous), Op zoek naar nieuwe spiritualiteit, spec. issue of *Civis Mundi*, vol. 26 no. 2, juni 1987.

Abram, D., The Perceptual Implications of Gaia, in: *The Ecologist*, 1985, vol. 15 no. 3, p. 96-104.

Abram, D., Merleau-Ponty and the Voice of the Earth, in: *Environmental Ethics*, vol. 10 no. 2, Summer 1988, p. 101-121.

Boerwinkel, H. W. J., Natuurbeleving, -waardering en -betrokkenheid, in: K. van Koppen e. a. (red.) 1984, p. 57-69.

Bulhof, I. N., *Naar een postmoderne spiritualiteit?* Oratie Leiden, 1992.

Bulhof, I. N., Filosofie en spiritualiteit; Een pleidooi voor een contemplatieve filosofie, in: *Streven*, oct. 1993, p. 788-803.

Carter, R. E., The Harmonious Person, in: *The Trumpeter*, vol. 8 no. 3, Summer 1991, p. 118-123.

Duintjer, O. D., Over natuur, vervreemding en heelwording, in: W. Achterberg en W. Zweers (red.) 1984, p. 189-208.

Duintjer, O. D., Spiritualiteit en de maatschappelijke wedren naar eindeloze expansie, in: *Civis Mundi*, vol. 24 no. 4, oct. 1985, p. 162-168.

Duintjer, O. D., Het belang van nieuwe spiritualiteit in een expansieve maatschappij, in: B. Nagel (red.) *Maken en Breken; over productie en spiritualiteit*, Kok/Agora, Kampen, 1988, p. 17-47.

Griffin, D. R. (Ed.), *Spirituality and Society; Postmodern Visions*, State Univ. of New-York Press, 1988.

Huxley, A., *The Perennial Philosophy*, Chatto and Windus, London 1946.

Krishnamurti, J., and D. Bohm, *The Ending of Time; Thirteen Dialogues*, Gollancz, London, 1985.

Needleman, J., *A Sense of the Cosmos; the encounter of modern science and ancient truth*, Dutton, New-York, 1976.

Schumacher, E. F., *A guide for the perplexed*, Cape, London, 1977 (*Gids voor de verdoolden*, Ambo, Baarn, 1977).

Shepard, P., Ecology and Man: a Viewpoint, in: R. Disch (Ed.) 1970, p. 56-67.

Steenbergen, B. van, Humanisme en het nieuwe religieuze bewustzijn, in: P. B. Cliteur en D.J. van Houten (red.), *Humanisme; Theorie en Praktijk*, De Tijdstroom, Utrecht, 1993, p. 171-183.

Waayman, K., Raakvlakken tussen natuurwetenschap en mystiek, in: *Wending*, vol. 39 no. 8, okt. 1984, p. 501-510.

Waayman, K. (red.), *Milieuspiritualiteit*, Titus Brandsma Instituut, Nijmegen, 1994 (student reader).

Watts, A., The world is your body, in: R. Disch (Ed.) 1970, p. 181-186.

Wit, H. de, *Contemplatieve Psychologie*, Kok/Agora, Kampen, 1987.

Zweers, W.,Varianten van ecologische ervaring, in: W. Achterberg en W. Zweers (red.) 1986, p. 19-73.

Zweers, W., Ecologische spiritualiteit als uitweg uit productiedenken, in: B. Nagel (red.) 1988, p. 210-235.

Technology

Achterhuis, H., *De illusie van groen; over milieucrisis en de fixatie op de techniek*, De Balie, Amsterdam, 1992.

Achterhuis, H., (red.), *De maat van de techniek*, Ambo, Baarn, 1992.

Achterhuis, H., *Natuur tussen mythe en techniek*, Ambo, Baarn, 1995.

Boers, C., Natuur in techniek en wetenschap, in: K. van Koppen e. a. (red.) 1984, p. 45-57.

Ellul, J., *The Technological Society*, Vintage Books, New-York, 1964.

Heidegger, M., *Die Technik und die Kehre*, Neske, Pfullingen, 1962 (*De techniek en de ommekeer*, Lannoo, Tielt, 1973).

Kockelkoren, P., (red.), *Boven de groene zoden; Een filosofische benadering van milieu, wetenschap en techniek*, Uitgeverij Jan van Arkel, Utrecht, 1990.

Kockelkoren, P., Naar een technische intimiteit met de dingen, in: *Wijsgerig Perspectief op Maatschappij en Wetenschap*, vol. 34 no. 6, 1993/94, p. 187-193.

Smits, M., De onduurzaamheid van duurzame techniek, in: *Wijsgerig Perspectief op Maatschappij en Wetenschap*, vol. 34 no. 6, 1993/94, p. 193-201.

Vergragt, Ph. J., Ecologische duurzaamheid en technologie, in: M. Mentzel, (red.), *Milieubeleid normatief bezien*, Stenfert Kroese, Leiden, 1993, p. 107-123.

Vermeersch, E., Weg van het wtk-bestel: onze toekomstige samenleving, in: (Anonymous), *Het Milieu: denkbeelden voor de* 21e eeuw, Commissie Lange Termijn Milieubeleid, Kerckebosch, Zeist, 1990.

Wal, G. A. van der, Geen maken aan. Reflecties op de technologische samenleving vanuit de ethiek, in: B. Nagel (red.) *Maken en Breken; over productie en spiritualiteit*, Kok/Agora, Kampen, 1988, p. 139-162.

Wal, G. A. van der, Technologie en ecologische crisis, in: W. Zweers (red.) 1991, p. 209-236 (with comments by P. Tijmes and M. Hilhorst)

Theology, Religion

Altner, G., (Hrsg.) *Ökologische Theologie; Perspektiven zur Orientierung*, Stuttgart, 1989.

Berry, T., *The Dream of the Earth*, Sierra Club Books, San Francisco, 1988.

Birch, C., W. Eakin and J. B. MacDaniel (Eds.), *Liberating Life; Contemporary Approaches to Ecological Theology*, Orbis Books, Maryknoll, New-York, 1990.

Cobb, J. Jr., Ecology, Science and Religion: Toward a Postmodern Worldview, in: Griffin, D. R. (Ed.), *The Reenchantment of Science; Postmodern Proposals*, State University of New-York Press, Albany, 1988 p. 99-115.

Dijk, P. van, Theologisch-anthropologische reflecties aangaande het milieuvraagstuk, in: W. Zweers (red.) 1991, p. 57-63.

Ferré, F., Religious World Modelling and Postmodern Science, in: D. R. Griffin (Ed.) 1988 (see above), p. 87-99.

Halkes, C.J.M., *...en alles zal worden herschapen; Gedachten over de heelwording van de schepping in het spanningsveld tussen natuur en cultuur*, Ten Have, Baarn, 1990.

Hargrove, E. (Ed.), *Religion and the Environmental Crisis*, Univ. of Georgia Press, Athens, 1986.

Haught, J., The Emergent Environment and the Problem of Cosmic Purpose, in: *Environmental Ethics*, vol. 8 no. 2, Summer 1986, p. 139-151.

Houtman, C., *Wereld en tegenwereld; Mens en milieu in de Bijbel/Mens en milieu en de Bijbel*, Ten Have, Baarn, 1982.

Irrgang, B., *Christliche Umweltethik; eine Einführung*, Reinhardt, München, 1992.

Liedke, G., *Im Bauch des Fisches. Ökologische Theologie*, Kreuz Verlag, Stuttgart, 1979.

MacDaniel, J., Christian Spirituality as Openness to Fellow Creatures, in: *Environmental Ethics*, vol. 8 no. 1, Spring 1986, p. 33-47.

MacDonagh, S., *To care for the Earth; a call to a new theology*, Chapman, London, 1986.

MacFague, S., *Models of God. Theology for an Ecological Nuclear Age*, 1987 (*Modellen voor God*, De Horstink, Amersfoort, 1991).

MacFague, S., *The Body of God: An Ecological Theology*, Fortress Press, Minneapolis, 1993/SCM Press, London, 1993.

Manenschijn, G., *Geplunderde aarde, getergde hemel; Ontwerp voor een christelijke milieu-ethiek*, Ten Have, Baarn, 1988.

Moltmann, J. *Gott in der Schöpfung; Ökologische Schöpfungslehre*, Kaiser, München, 1985.

Needleman, J., *Lost Christianity; A Journey of Rediscovery to the Center of Christian Experience*, Doubleday, Garden City, 1980 (*Het verloren Christendom*, Ankh/Hermes, Deventer, 1985).

Perk, N. van der, *Christendom en ecologische crisis; Vervreemding en bevrijding*, Inst. voor Theoretische Biologie, Leiden, 1985.

Perk, N. van der, *De aarde en haar kruis; Over Christendom en milieucrisis*, Kok/Agora, Kampen, 1988.

Perk, N. van der, Natuurbeeld-kritiek of maatschappijkritiek?, in: W. Achterberg (red.) 1989, p. 160-177.

Scherer, G., *Welt – Natur oder Schöpfung?* Wissenschaftliche Buchgesellschaft, Darmstadt, 1990.

Schuurman, F., Religieus-wijsgerige achtergronden van het milieuprobleem, in: K. van Koppen e. a. (red.) 1985, p. 23-32.

Whitehead, A. N., *De dynamiek van de religie (Religion in the Making)*, vert. door en met commentaar van J. van der Veken, Kok/Agora, Kampen, 1988 (1926).

Wiskerke, N., New Age-holisme en Scheppingstheologie – visies op mens en natuur, in: *Holisme en New Age-bewustzijn; fenomenologische, theologische en ecologische aspecten van een nieuw wereldbeeld*, Universiteit Brabant, Theologische Faculteit, Tilburg, 1986, p. 139-211.

Wood, H. W., Modern Pantheism as an Approach to Environmental Ethics, in: *Environmental Ethics*, vol. 7 no. 2, Summer 1985, p. 151-165.

Zweers, W., Christendom en ecologisch perspectief, in: *De Ronde Tafel*, no. 17, aug./sept. 1987, p. 34-39.

Miscellaneous

Achterberg, W., Toekomstige generaties: intuïtief en contra-intuïtief, in: W. Achterberg (red.) 1989, p. 85-96.

Armstrong-Buck, S., Whitehead's metaphysical system as a foundation for environmental ethics, in: *Environmental Ethics*, vol. 8 no. 3, Fall 1986, p. 241-261.

Armstrong-Buck, S., What Process Philosophy Can Contribute to the Land Ethic and Deep Ecology, in: *The Trumpeter*, vol. 8 no. 1, Winter 1991, p. 29-35.

Bien, G.,T. Gil und J. Wilke (Hrsg.), *"Natur" im Umbruch; Zur Diskussion des Naturbegriffs in Philosophie, Naturwissenschaft und Kunsttheorie*, Fromman-Holzboog, Stuttgart, 1994.

Böhme, G., *Natürlich Natur; Über Natur im Zeitalter ihrer technischen Reproduzierbarkeit*, Ed. Suhrkamp, NF 680, Frankfurt am Main, 1992.

Callenbach, E., *Ecotopia; A novel about ecology, people and politics in 1999*, and *Ecotopia emerging*, resp. Pluto Press, London, 1978 (1975) and Banyan Tree, New-York, 1981.

Cowell, M., Ecological Restoration and Environmental Ethics, in: *Environmental Ethics*, vol. 15 no. 1, Spring 1993, p. 19-33 (over natuurontwikkeling).

Groot, W. T. de, Metaphysics for Rural Policy: the partnership view of man and nature applied to the Western Dutch Lowlands, in: J. Frouws and W. T. de Groot (Eds.), *Environment and Agriculture in the Netherlands*, Leiden/Wageningen, 1987.

Groot, W. T. de, Van waterwolf tot partner; het culturele aspect van het nieuwe waterbeleid, in: *Milieu; Tijdschrift voor Milieukunde*, vol. 2, 1987 no. 3, p. 84-87.

Keurs, W. J. ter, Naar een meer maatschappelijke natuurbescherming, in: K. van Koppen e. a. (red.) 1984, p. 132-142.

Kockelkoren, P., *Van een plantaardig naar een plant-waardig bestaan; ethische aspecten van biotechnologie bij planten*, Den Haag, Ministerie van Landbouw, Natuurbeheer en Visserij, 1993.

Koppen, K. van, De milieubeweging tussen Verlichting en Romantiek. in: K. van Koppen e. a. (red.) 1984, p. 119-132.

Kwee Swan-Liat, Wonen en werken op de kleine aarde, in: W. Achterberg en W. Zweers (red.) 1986, p. 231-257.

Lemaire, T., *Twijfel aan Europa; Zijn de intellectuelen de vijanden van de Europese cultuur?*, Ambo, Baarn, 1990.

MacDaniel, J., Physical Matter as Creative and Sentient, in: *Environmental Ethics*, vol. 5 no. 4, Winter 1983, p. 291-318.

Rodman, J., The Liberation of Nature?, in: *Inquiry*, vol. 20, Spring 1977, p. 83-131.

Roose, F. de, Utilisme en natuurbehoud, in: *Filosofie en Praktijk*, vol. 9 no. 3, sept. 1988, p. 128-143.

About the Authors

Prof. Gerrit Huizer is director of the Third World Centre of the Catholic University Nijmegen, the Netherlands.

Dr. Petran Kockelkoren is researcher at the department of Systematic Philosophy, University of Twente, the Netherlands.

Dr. Vandana Shiva is atomic scientist and conservationist/environmentalist, India.

Dr. Henk Verhoog is assistant professor in the philosophy of biology, Institute of Evolutionary and Ecological Sciences, Leiden University, the Netherlands.

Dr. Frans Verkleij is researcher at the Department of Ecological Agriculture at the Agricultural University of Wageningen, and studies theology at the University of Utrecht, the Netherlands.

Ir. Rob P. Witte is consultant in ecological agriculture, the Netherlands.

Wim Zweers teaches and publicizes in the field of environmental philososphy.